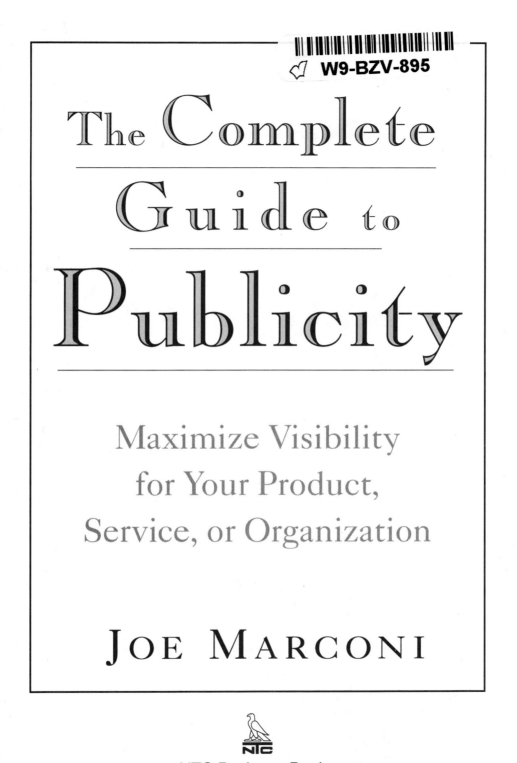

The Complete

Guide to

Publicity

Maximize Visibility
for Your Product,
Service, or Organization

JOE MARCONI

NTC Business Books
NTC/Contemporary Publishing Group

Library of Congress Cataloging-in-Publication Data

Marconi, Joe.
    The complete guide to publicity: maximize visibility for your
product, service, or organization / Joe Marconi.
        p.   cm.
    Includes bibliographical references (p.) and index.
    ISBN 0-8442-0090-5 (cloth).—ISBN 0-8442-0091-3 (pbk.)
    1. Publicity.   I. Title.
HM263.M2743   1998
659—dc21   98-39670
                                                          CIP

Interior design by Precision Graphics

Published by NTC Business Books
A division of NTC/Contemporary Publishing Group, Inc.
4255 West Touhy Avenue, Lincolnwood (Chicago), Illinois 60646-1975 U.S.A.
Copyright © 1999 by Joe Marconi
Printed in the United States of America
International Standard Book Number: 0-8442-0090-5 (cloth)
                                                          0-8442-0091-3 (paper)
99 00 01 02 03 04 MV 18 17 16 15 14 13 12 11 10 9 8 7 6 5 4 3 2 1

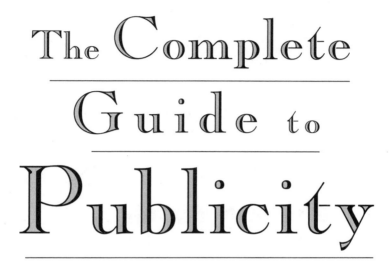

The Complete
Guide to
Publicity

For Todd and Kristin and Emily
and for Karin

Contents

Introduction

Few people in business would question the value of recognition. To be recognized often carries the suggestion of importance: the best-known brands are often regarded as the best brands; the most talked-about show in town is the "must-see" show. But are they the best, or have they just had the benefit of some very good publicity?

A comment that has survived the years and straddled the space of everyday life and business is: "I don't care what people say about me, just as long as they get my name right."

For a generation or more, that message seemed to embody the strategy, tactic, and objective of being noticed. *Notice* was what it was about. Bring a subject to the public's attention, make the subject well known, and success would follow.

Well, maybe, but then again, maybe not.

Publicity can be a powerful tool to both create and tear down a product, company, name, or reputation. It can both create and change an image or perception. How much today's technology has altered both the methods and the impact of publicity is an area of great concern to individuals, small independent enterprises, and great corporations and institutions alike. The effects of "word of mouth" may still be of singular importance, but when two heads leaning over a back fence or over a cup of coffee have been replaced by millions of "mouths" on the Internet at any given time of the day or night, the rules of the publicity process have clearly and dramatically changed.

From the rich and famous, the moguls, to the wanna-bes and kitchen-table entrepreneurs, publicity has always been a key that could unlock the door to so much. It was both the plan and the program, and sometimes it was the objective in and of itself.

Planners of the PTA fun fair, the struggling community theater group, the local hospital, small businesses as well as *Fortune 500* companies, all know that publicity means notice: awareness, attention, and interest, all of which can help pave the way to increased sales, support, or opportunities for success on any number of levels. Recruiting efforts, the price of a company's stock, creating or increasing brand loyalty, public acceptance, or a crisis-management strategy all turn largely on the effectiveness of publicity.

How it's done, what it costs, and the theory and practice of devising and managing an effective publicity program form the basis of this book.

Even before we are aware of it, we are eager for attention. As we get older, humility and the social graces usually temper these desires, although the hope for recognition is still an ever-present characteristic of human nature. Business takes a more formalized approach, recognizing that a product, name, service, or company—any type of venture—can succeed only if the public knows about it and, perhaps more important, must act upon that knowledge by buying or otherwise supporting what the subject entity has to sell.

Publicity—*the desire or need to publicize a subject*—thus becomes not only a quality inherent in all of us, but also a process essential to the successful management and marketing of a business venture on virtually any level.

The legendary Howard Hughes is said to have hired publicists to keep his name *out* of the press, but even that bit of information became a part of an ongoing flow of publicity that helped an image, a reputation, and the Hughes name (or brand) evolve into a very marketable commodity. The so-called bashful billionaire was also a notable exception (if not the sole exception) when it comes to an avowed desire to avoid even the most favorable publicity.

Just spell the name right? Clearly there are some people who sought publicity who would rather the public not have tracked their *every* move. The oil company that wants people to know its brand by name, logo, slogan, and jingle but would prefer that when one of its tankers is responsible for an oil spill, the headline writers discreetly treat the brand as if it were a generic. Tobacco companies would prefer that the public identify their particular brands with their advertising phrases such as cool, smooth, and rich tasting, not with lawsuits linking their products to diseases. The late pop singer, we would assume, would have liked to be remembered for his music and his high-profile efforts on behalf of environmental causes, not his high-profile divorces, drunk-driving arrests, and much-publicized reports of fuel hoarding during an energy crisis. Community hospitals want to be known for the lives they save, not for the seemingly rare lawsuit involving a person turned away.

The answer, then, is no: any publicity is *not* good publicity. Only good publicity is good publicity.

This book is for individuals and corporations, for products, services, associations, organizations, franchises, not-for-profit groups, and even those enterprises that do, in fact, hope to make a profit. It is a series of examples and a step-by-step guide for any and all who might be interested in developing and implementing a plan for effectively generating a maximum amount of good publicity.

For their contributions to this effort, thanks to Richard Hagle, Jamie Born, Helen Kensick, Golin/Harris Communications, Bender Browning Dolby & Sanderson, Lonny Bernardi, and Rich Girod and, again, a special thanks to Karin Gottschalk Marconi for being the glue in the last six books.

The Complete
Guide to
Publicity

1

Publicity: Definitions and Distinctions

WHAT IT IS AND WHAT IT ISN'T

Simply put, publicity is about publicizing a subject, creating attention, getting notice. Is publicity about talking to the press? Yes, but it is much more than that. The word *publicity* itself, in normal usage, implies getting *positive* attention, as in *"We need to generate publicity for the upcoming event."* Indeed, the title of this book, without saying so, implies that the text is a guide to getting *good* publicity.

When we read on a magazine cover that a particular subject is "the hottest game in town," do we stop to wonder how the magazine's editors came to know this?

Who is it exactly that has determined someone to be worthy of the designation "most popular" or "fastest rising"?

Every time we hear a company referred to as "the next Microsoft" or "the next generation's IBM" or hear a product touted as the "next Cabbage Patch doll" or "Tickle Me Elmo" or a rising entrepreneur described as "a young Ross Perot," every time we read that a performer is being hailed as the "new Elvis" or is compared to Frank Sinatra or the Beatles, we are being exposed to publicity for a new entity that seeks to raise our expectations and attach a

1

higher than usual level of potential success. While few that are the object of such comparisons ever come close to achieving such comparable success, the technique is still the most commonly used. How it is used is one of the subjects this book will explore.

Be aware, however, that not only is there such a thing as *bad* publicity, but also bad publicity is easier to get as well as more difficult to undo and will, more often than not, have a more lasting effect than similar positive news. Therefore, the publicist's efforts must be geared to getting *good* publicity, while avoiding those missteps that may result in *bad* publicity.

The term *publicity* is often used synonymously and interchangeably with the terms *press agentry, promotion,* and *public relations.* This is a mistake. While it is not unusual for functions to overlap, each is a discipline or process with its own distinctions.

Publicity is about creating and managing information aimed at one or more targeted audiences in the hope of influencing opinions and decisions.

Is publicity "hype": essentially drumbeating and touting your message, cause, product, or issue? It can be used as such, but the terms are not synonymous. The publicist's skill and effort are important in that, unlike other forms of communication, one's first response to an item of information is often the strongest or most lasting impression, which can be extremely challenging to override or change.

Press agentry is a function of servicing the media, whether initiating or responding to a contact, such as acting as a press secretary to a public official. In this context, managing publicity can be virtually an art form. Responding to a single inquiry can generate tremendous attention—positive or negative—or the response or exchange of comments could be used at a later time, perhaps as part of a larger or even unrelated story. It could also become part of an official file or record, viewed by reporters, researchers, students, or historians in any number of ways. Think of it in much the same way as your old schoolteacher's telling you that something would become "a part of your permanent record that would follow you all through life."

Press agents, unlike publicists, are the ones most frequently accused of trying to "manage" news or to put a particular "spin" on a subject or piece of information. In the 1980s the terms *spin control* and *spin doctor* became part of the public's everyday vocabulary. They were used as glib and usually disparaging references applied to the people and process where "working the press" involved attempts to dramatically shape opinions—often by means of reshaping or even rewriting information from the form in which it was originally presented.

Press agents are often called upon to do *damage control*, attempting to reverse or modify the effects of a negative comment or story. In earlier generations, powerful people in government, on Wall Street, and in various lofty corporate positions would often be credited with having the power to "kill" a story, to keep anything that might reflect negatively about their interests from ever being printed. In the modern world such situations are virtually impossible. The hunger for even trivial celebrity data precludes keeping a good bit of gossip under wraps, and even claims of "national security" have not discouraged members of the media from reporting information.

Promotion has become a very broad area itself. Promoting a book, a film, a product, a company, or an event typically includes generating a high volume of publicity. Historically, to receive a great amount of publicity was to heighten awareness, and that was considered good. Increasingly, because modern media have focused on their subjects with a greater intensity than in earlier times, a high degree of publicity has been characterized as "hype" and has raised expectations to sometimes unrealistic levels. This then creates a "publicity backlash" in which greater attention is paid to the publicity campaign than to the subject itself. Media that are so hungry for information have helped to create an environment where hype is increasingly common.

A promotion can also be an event or a device. A celebrity appearance, a game, a contest, sweepstakes, a concert, or an exhibition can all be examples of promotions. The category also describes items carrying the subject's logo, brand name, or signature, such as tote bags, T-shirts, pens, coffee mugs, and key rings, though they typically fall short of generating considerable publicity by themselves. There are exceptions to this, of course, such as highly sought-after shirts with an especially popular radio station's call letters or logo, a popular performer's concert "tour" jacket, or a bumper sticker tied in to a contest or other type of prize giveaway. Increasingly companies are creating entire catalogs of branded merchandise, from clothing to cookie jars, that once would have been free promotional items to raise brand awareness. The items sell for significant amounts—sometimes higher than the cost of the same-quality merchandise *without* the brand logo—and are regarded as both desirable and reflecting personal preferences as well as pop culture. They also, not incidentally, publicize the subject.

Public relations is the wide field and the umbrella term under which publicity is typically a part or function. But public relations includes many non-publicity-related functions, such as lobbying and governmental relations, investor relations, speechwriting, and the production and publication of literature, such as annual and interim reports, brochures, fact sheets, research studies, biographical and historical data, statistical reports, and human resource–related materials, such as employee handbooks, newsletters, posters, workshops, seminars and meetings, and other components, the objective of which may or may not involve the generating of publicity.

Publicity is also not advertising. Advertisers buy time and/or space to present their messages to generate or promote awareness of their subject. The advantage of advertising over other forms of information dissemination is the ability to exercise sole control over content, timing, and placement, as well as the frequency of the message's appearance (as often as the ad budget allows).

The disadvantage is that there is a tremendous amount of clutter—the public perception that there are far too many ads—which creates a barrier to the audience's favorably receiving or accepting the message. Another disadvantage is the cost. Creative executions alone can run into six or seven figures, and media costs—the actual price of purchasing time or space—can be staggering and prohibiting to many budgets. Add to that the fees for recognizable figures—models, politicians, entertainers, or other celebrities—and the cost again soars. But, by far, the greatest disadvantage to advertising over publicity or public relations is its lack of the credibility that comes from having a seemingly authoritative, objective entity (the writer, editor, commentator, or reporter) showcase a subject versus the subject's having to pay to toot its own horn. Someone once described advertising as "publicity that you pay for." That might be a bit too simplistic.

Why are these distinctions important to know?

One reason is personnel related. If a company, a firm, an association, or any other entity is seeking someone to handle publicity, candidates—be it a person or an agency—should have a clear understanding of what the function includes. A seasoned public relations practitioner may be a terrific strategist, lobbyist, event planner, or writer but may not necessarily have any experience or skill in dealing with the media, the public, trade associations, or whoever/whatever the target audiences might be.

THE PUBLICIST: ETHICS, IMAGINATION, ENERGY

Publicists are *salespeople.*

Any good salesperson knows that success doesn't come from sitting back and waiting for the phone to ring. A publicist understands that a well-crafted press release, distributed to a good media list, will rarely be enough to generate a significant amount of good publicity. That is only a part of the process. Just as the salesperson cultivates a territory, the publicist's environment should be studied and preconditioned, the approach carefully developed. Also as in sales, in the words of the seasoned motivational speakers, you have to: *(1) tell them what you're going to tell them; (2) tell them what you want them to hear; and (3) tell them what you just told them.*

A message to be received under the best of all circumstances must be presented to an audience ready and willing to hear it, well stated and with enough consistency and follow-through to make certain that its impact and effects register.

Sell the story. Make the calls and follow through.

Truth has always been included in the list of important concerns when it comes to dealing with the public, although, as incongruous as it may seem, people seem to want to keep redefining exactly what it means to be truthful. Since the cynicism of the 1970s, references to telling the truth have become obligatory and have virtually taken on an irrelevance similar to the unreadable microscopic warnings on most medicine bottles.

Surveys say that most members of the public don't trust most businesses, most agencies of government, and one another. Still, for the publicist, trust and adherence to an ethical standard must be respected and practiced, because to do otherwise is to set oneself up to even greater charges of attempting to mislead or color the truth.

The simplest rule is this: *Be honest and straightforward with the public because it is easier than trying to remember which lies you told to whom and what might come back to bite you in the rear end.*

It is reasonable to conclude that by the time America reached the threshold of the 21st century, the bar had been moved when it came to the definition of truth, civility, and ethics. A typical day's news coverage—local or national—and a wide variety of radio and TV talk shows are likely to include people issuing a stream of insults and making offensive comments. The old rules of courtesy and etiquette seem no longer to apply. Prominent spokespersons casually call their rivals and critics liars or worse. Clearly, when attempting to attract the attention of the media, to get the public to notice and to make an impression that stands out from the hundreds of other impressions formed in an average day, the trend seems to be *the more outspoken—and outrageous—the better.*

What does the fact that people behave badly in public say about the rules of what is now acceptable behavior in business and the media? What impact does this behavior have on a publicist's attempts to aggressively generate interest in a subject? Does it mean that all bets are off when it comes to courtesy, or what business used to describe as appropriate behavior?

Probably not. It does, however, suggest that through the expansion of so-called attack ads and references comparing a company or product with other companies and products, the public's tolerance level has grown to where openly insulting competitors, questioning their ethics and integrity, has become commonplace. Be aware that once such a tone has been set for a competitive exchange, the rules of engagement virtually demand equal levels of aggression. That is to say, the side that refuses to return the fire may be regarded as staying out of the mud but is then left with the stains the mud has created. In short, if you shoot first, expect to have your fire returned, and be prepared. If you are the object of the attack, be prepared with your strongest possible response, while trying to maintain as much dignity as possible, mindful of the long-term impact of such an exchange on your public image.

In the 1988 campaign for president of the United States, Democrat candidate Michael Dukakis was attacked as soft on criminals and "too liberal" in most other areas. Candidate Dukakis, then the governor of Massachusetts, a soft-spoken and seemingly emotionless man who was determined to wage a dignified campaign, chose to let his record speak for itself and to "take the high road," refusing to attack his attackers. He did not want his campaign organization to mount either an attack or a counterattack campaign.

The result was the public's getting an impression that the candidate was indeed too soft and perhaps lacked the strength necessary to meet the challenges of such a demanding job. When the votes were counted, Dukakis's defeat by George Bush was not by a merely decisive margin; it was a humiliating margin.

It was the attacks in ads and speeches that both *defined and pursued* the candidate, and his refusal to respond seemed to validate the attacks. While it is difficult to advocate an attack approach—and clearly, research surveys indicate public disdain for such a tactic—it is more difficult to deny its effectiveness.

In business and corporate campaigns, the same rules apply. If a rival or competitor attacks, and the attacks go unanswered or are not obliterated, the attack message tends to stick and do residual damage over time.

Perhaps taking a "modified" high road means not attacking first, but merely responding aggressively to an attack. This is a good approach. The downside of waiting for someone to fire a first shot is the possibility that the damage done will be beyond recovery.

In 1997 two hotel chains were engaged in fierce competition for the purchase of a third chain. In interviews with reporters and industry analysts, as well as in ads in major newspapers, the two rival companies each accused the other of misrepresenting both its own and its competitor's offers, and each attacked its rival for disseminating false and misleading—if not outright fraudulent—information, following questionable financial practices, and lying to shareholders.

Whew! And this was only over the acquisition of some hotels! Fortunately, neither group's CEO challenged the other to a duel, although it looked at times as if it might come to that. In the securities analyst community, many shook their heads at such conduct unbecoming to otherwise high-minded organizations.

Is this behavior appropriate? Is it in the best interests of the shareholders or the industry to which it brings attention?

Again, probably not. But what is the responsibility of the publicist who carries the message and who often has a voice in creating the strategy or approach? Some might claim it is little more than an "All's fair" or "Whatever it takes" response to a challenge. As times become increasingly more competitive, responses become more aggressive. A debate seems appropriate over whether or not aggressive must be the same as uncivilized or unethical. Unfortunately, the definition of what is ethical seems to keep getting broader.

Increasingly, the statement is offered that "The issue was decided in the media" or "The two sides argued their case in the media." These comments are clearly in reference to attempts to use public opinion to win support for a position that will then be decided in a boardroom, by a shareholder election, or in court.

Are the publicists who "argue" these positions pursuing a fact-based, ethical course, or trying to merely manipulate emotions at any price?

The answer is, it depends not only on the issue and the circumstances, but also on who is in the role of publicist.

A woman who sued a political figure was neither a sympathetic nor persuasive person—nor were her attorneys when they met the media on her behalf. It was only after the woman's legal team engaged a spokesperson—a publicist—to appear on talk shows, newscasts, and interview shows and to issue a series of stories and anecdotes that sought to better *define her case* that public opinion seemed to begin shifting in her favor.

Was this bringing forward a case on its merits, or was it aggressively manipulating coverage—publicity—to gain momentum and support? Practitioners who support the woman will say it is both, and it is both justified and ethical.

Lawyers, after years of criticizing other lawyers for seeking public attention and holding such behavior as undignified, are increasingly acting as publicists, appearing on TV and radio talk shows, both seeking and granting interviews, holding press conferences on the courthouse steps and out on their lawns—all in attempts to influence public opinion by generating publicity.

Woody Allen said there is a special floor in hell reserved for lawyers who appear on television. During the O. J. Simpson trials of the mid-1990s, it might have looked as if all available space would be spoken for. No morning, day, evening, or late night passed for some two years without one of the defendant's many lawyers appearing on one or more of the morning news shows, call-in shows, midday shows, evening news programs, prime-time magazine hours, syndicated "tabloid" shows, or late-night news and interview shows. Whether the objective was to influence the courts, sway prospective jurors, manipulate the media, or promote their myriad of books, tapes, and speaking engagements—and the lawyers' individual careers—the facts were obvious: publicity was being used in the most overt and aggressive ways to *define* the issues and aspects of the case, as well as to attempt to portray who were the good guys and the bad guys.

Do lawyers make good publicists?

Sometimes. Often the lawyers are the most informed parties to an issue in the public eye. But lawyers are also historically the absolute worst people to address issues that need to be contained— when large amounts of publicity may not be in the subject's best interests. Precisely because they *are* well informed, when they are unwilling or unable to answer questions or provide information, the subject company, product, individual, or issue is represented as uncooperative, not forthcoming, and, perhaps, even arrogant or attempting to conceal information. At such times professionals other than lawyers are far better spokespersons or front people.

Just as the terms to describe the publicity process are used interchangeably with other terms, so the terms to describe the publicity *person* are somewhat varied. Some people prefer to be called practitioners; others are spokespersons, advance people, or information officers. None prefer to be called *flacks*.

The term *flack* is to the publicist what *shrink* is to the psychologist. It's disparaging and dismissive, though most publicists seem to be able to shrug it off, laugh it off, or at least not take it too seriously.

But it is important for a publicist to understand that business or media people who characterize publicists as flacks may be trying to convey, however good-naturedly, their lack of respect or appreciation for the process or profession, perhaps reflecting opinions and perceptions formed by experience.

Some publicists will tell clients, "I'll get you on the cover of *Fortune*" or "I'll get your story in the *Wall Street Journal*."

Note to clients: *Don't buy it.* It's not possible. Such placements are not for sale and cannot be guaranteed.

Note to publicists: *Don't promise it.* Saying so may make a client smile for a while, but when reality kicks in and the story doesn't materialize, the publicist likely gets fired, and the profession is left with a black eye.

The best media outlets (and even many of the less desirable spots) may offer ad space for sale, but they don't offer their covers or editorial space for the asking by publicists. And publicists who are confident of their abilities or of the strength of their contacts also know that a good story—or even a mediocre item of interest—can be *brought to the attention* of the media, but the decision on whether or not the item gets time or space is that of the editor.

True, sometimes trades are made. Companies or agencies with access to highly desirable, newsworthy subjects will offer exclusivity in exchange for some notice being granted as well to a less desirable client or product. The big movie studios used to do this all the time. Some publications do in fact give favored editorial space or attention to their advertisers. But the ethical standards of virtually all major media outlets are beyond such "trades," and ethical publicists know this.

It was often said of President Richard Nixon's White House, for example, that it was run by flacks and spin doctors. Perhaps it is not necessary to note that such remarks were not intended as compliments. The remarks were supported by documented, repeated instances of dishonest, dishonorable, and unethical behavior with regard to the management of information. Which is to say, they lied.

John Anthony Maltese, a professor of political science at the University of Georgia, on the subject of spin control, noted that "manipulating the media and emphasizing style—often at the expense of substance—are now thought to be essential parts of modern presidential power. As Richard Nixon wrote in his memoirs, '[modern presidents] must try to master the art of manipulating, not only to win in politics, but in order to further the causes and programs they believe in . . .'"

Or they can hire someone to do it. The point, as well as the issue, can be shifted to apply to situations somewhat closer to home than the office of president of the United States. Wealthy or celebrated people, such as Ross Perot, Donald Trump, or O. J. Simpson, are credited with possessing an ability to manipulate those around them and the media for their own advantage. Some publicists use children, hardship cases, pretty girls, or appealing animals to attract cameras and draw attention. In this way, they are also manipulating the media.

In order to be consistently effective, a publicist must have the eye, ear, goodwill, and current phone numbers of media people, many of whom are suspicious, distrustful, or even disdainful of those who seek their attention and interest on a regular basis. They frequently extend these feelings to persons representing those who seek attention.

The publicist's job is made significantly easier when his or her ethics and integrity are beyond reproach. This desired status comes from the publicist's having created relationships with members of the media, the professions, and the community and from building a reputation. Typically, relative strangers who ask us to trust them at first sight are those less likely to be trusted. A history or track record is necessary. Ethics and integrity are rarely assumed, and the nature of the media is to be wary of those who come asking for coveted radio or television time or print space to advance their own causes without charge.

Reputations can be built quickly by showing some imagination—by following fundamentally established procedures but in an original way that produces positive results.

An example is the matter of the securities exchange that wanted to generate some positive publicity for itself, raising its level of awareness to the public while at the same time hoping to neutralize criticism from rival exchanges and a couple of high-profile curmudgeonly columnists. The exchange leadership considered calling a news conference to refute gossip and tell its own side of the story. One problem with this idea was that there was no "news" as such to justify a news conference, and the occasion would largely serve only to revisit subjects that were not in the best interests of the exchange to keep alive.

The exchange's publicity person instead devised the idea of sending a short note to reporters, announcing that the exchange would be having a "press update." No major announcements were anticipated. It was just an opportunity for key officials of the institution to meet with members of the press, around a conference table, in shirtsleeves, with coffee and doughnuts, everything on the record and no subject off-limits.

The approach had a certain seductive element to reporters. It was an opportunity to speak face-to-face with high-level executives who might normally meet only infrequently with the press. Second, knowing that rival media were also invited to attend, reporters who might consider not participating had to be concerned about missing something that might then be literally handed to a competitor. The "everything-on-the-record/no-subject-off-limits" notice also underscored both the openness of the exchange leaders and the presumption that such behavior would elicit an appropriately courteous response from participating media people. Reporters were being offered an invitation to add important names to their personal files—people who might not have been willing sources had it not been for the relaxed, friendly, candid atmosphere of the session.

The event was a success. Eleven reporters attended, filing 16 separate stories over the week following the session. The publicist knew that just the existence of the exchange and its desire for good publicity was not sufficient justification for a "news conference."

An *event*, however, that offered access, information, and an opportunity to develop future story material and sources did prove worthy of media attention.

In stark contrast is the example involving a wealthy, prominent couple whose young daughter had been brutally murdered, apparently in their home, while the family slept. The story was of national interest. Media at all levels wanted photos, footage, comments, and interviews.

With the murderer at large, an investigation ongoing, and persistent rumors indicating that the murdered child's parents were among those persons under suspicion, the couple hired a well-known, high-profile public relations firm.

Rather than serve as a helpful center to provide information and respond with quiet dignity to those reporters whom the couple knew, the sudden appearance of a contingent of publicists on the scene, during a still early period of mourning, sent a message to the press and the public that the couple appeared more interested in preserving and promoting what they perceived was the couple's own image than in finding the killer.

In this instance, negative publicity—indeed, the very idea of having it become publicly known that the parents had engaged someone to manage their personal publicity under such circumstances—only compounded the tragedy of the child's murder.

A publicist is most effective when the focus is kept on the subject, not when the publicist *becomes* the subject. In this instance, the matter exploded unnecessarily into a tabloid event, included in sketches of the case for many months to follow.

A publicist operating discreetly as a part of the family lawyer's inner circle, or behind the scenes, in the role of family friend, might have been more successful in keeping the focus away from the couple during their earliest period of grief.

In some cases publicity does indeed involve the practice of *limiting* the attention that is afforded. But that is not to say the publicist is blocking information from being shared or is lying or misleading the media or the public.

Lawyers offer lofty speeches on the need to protect their clients' rights and interests and to work their strategies, but a publicist must demonstrate a sense of ethics that is grounded in truthfulness and openness, or the resulting impression can be disastrous.

A publicist's ethics are rarely at issue when the news is good. It is more typically when the subject in question is negative that a company or client will be accused of attempting to "hide behind" a publicist, who is then regarded as less than forthcoming.

Consider this: the more positive information a publicist can provide, the greater the context in which good news can be regarded as building an image, reputation, awareness, and momentum. In crisis situations, this larger context helps frame negative news in such a way that it is only a part of the company's story and not *all* that the public knows of the client.

PUBLICITY AS PART OF THE LARGER MARKETING PLAN

The subject is a product, a company, a person, or an event, and the objective is to publicize it—*and that's all.* That's clear enough. But when publicity is just one component of a larger public relations or marketing effort, a lack of coordination can undercut the effectiveness of the publicity, as well as the overall program effort, and perhaps result in embarrassment.

For example, a good marketing plan will consider what competitors are doing and have done and factor this information into the plan's strategy and tactics. Statements in ads, brochures, or other documents referring to comparisons with competitors should be consistent with, reflected in, and supported by statements included in the publicity efforts.

Some companies will use separate agencies for advertising and public relations, with, on occasion, additional agencies tapped to handle events or governmental and shareholder affairs. Frequently, as illogical as it may seem, these agencies will act fully independent of one another, and their messages in content, tone, and timing may be—or at least may *appear* to be—inconsistent.

One division of a company may be trying to aggressively promote an event or a new product introduction, seemingly unaware that another division is competing for the same media attention during the same time frame. A reporter or editor may ask a question of the publicist for one division about the other's subject, only to be given the impression that the right hand doesn't know what the left hand is doing.

Sound ridiculous?

It happens every day in agencies and departments of government, franchise operations, and businesses both large and small. It can be an especially challenging problem in an environment in which management encourages fierce competition among divisions. Competition is fine, but a lack of coordination within a company, or among a group of companies under the same umbrella, is counterproductive.

Information is a publicist's essential tool. A publicist cannot effectively disseminate and manage information if he or she doesn't *have* the information. Before embarking on an effort to publicize a subject, a publicist must know where and how the subject fits into an overall plan; what, if anything, else is being presented relative to the same subject (advertising, direct mail, promotional literature, rack pieces or posters); and what, if anything, has been or is being done within the subject's "universe" that might affect the publicity or redirect interest in the subject.

Most people have heard about how the best-laid plans can go awry. Consider the potential for disaster that can result from not even being *aware* of the plans. To avoid disaster:

- Have a publicity plan.
- Determine if the publicity plan is a part of a larger public relations or marketing plan.

- If it is, make certain that the content and timing of your efforts are consistent with those of the other plans within your organization.

PUBLICITY BY OBJECTIVES: SETTING OBJECTIVES; CREATING THE PLAN

New York City public relations consultant Dorothy I. Doty suggests: "Don't even try to imitate someone else's publicity program. Whether yours is a deli in Queens or a multinational corporation, you must tailor your program to fit your company's specific goals, needs, personnel, geography, products, services, and style. Whatever it is, if it is part of your business, it is unique."

Well, yes and no.

Doty's position is correct in that the key point that will help you sell your message is whatever it is that's unique about your company, but some of the best ideas come from looking at what others, both inside and outside of your own industry, have done and asking what about that could be done better or how *you* might have handled it if it had been *your* program. This is something you would especially want to consider if the approach that you observed someone else taking turned out to be extremely successful. Be unique; be original, but don't dismiss a very good idea because someone else has done it. See how you might adapt it to your need.

Some companies hire publicists and take a position something like "OK, we're paying you—now get us publicity and make the product better known."

In fairness, this directive doesn't seem difficult to understand. All the company wants to do is get some publicity. It's not rocket science. Of course, the company could buy ad space to let its public know that it exists and what it does. Publicity, however, requires more to interest the media in a subject. Just existing isn't enough. The question the publicist needs to ask and answer is, *Why should the public want to know about this subject?*

What is a part of the answer, but without answering the *why,* there is no story. The publicist still needs to know as much as there is to know about the subject.

In advertising, the defining element of the subject of the ad is its USP—its *unique selling point*—what makes it different or noteworthy. A publicist must similarly identify such value in the subject at issue.

Good planning can involve several "first steps" which may be considered in differing order but each of which is no less important than the others. One is defining the subject of your publicity. This will sharpen your message. The more specific you can be, the more clearly focused your plan is likely to be. It is not necessary or even advisable to try to cover a large amount of information in a single story or placement. If there is value in who you are, what you have, and what you do, there will be room in the plan for the whole story to be told, albeit not in a single press release.

For example, if you are a midsize Midwestern manufacturer, determine first which entry on this list you want to publicize:

- your product
- your company
- your "family of products"
- your management
- an event tied to your product or company

If it so happens you are *not* a midsize Midwestern manufacturer, substitute what you are—restaurant, hospital, hair salon, accounting firm, entertainer, politician, sports team, trade association, or (<u>fill in the blank</u>)—and apply the same points for consideration.

Your *product* is that which you have to sell, even if you define it as your voice, knowledge, or talent, your presence or service, an event, or your cause. It is that which you offer for the consideration of your audience.

Your *company* is defined as the offering entity, apart from the product itself. While sometimes it might appear that the product defines the company, this may not ever or always be true.

Your *family of products* can be a grouping of related items, services, skills, or people that are each not necessarily less or greater than the others, and that the dictates of time, budgets, politics, and audience preferences have determined be represented in one message space. As its family of products, a music or record company might offer cassettes, CDs, records, laser discs, or videotapes all on the same subject. A financial services company may present a variety of mutual funds, unit investment trusts, annuities, or insurance plans all under the same banner. No one item is regarded as superior to the others.

Your *management* is defined as the decision-making entity behind the product or company. On occasion—Ford, Hilton, Marriott, and Forbes come to mind—the product, company, and management appear to be so enmeshed as to be all the same. They aren't. As the subject of your message, perhaps the person or people represented as management is the founder of the company or inventor of the product. This person may or may not still be in charge. Perhaps the management is newly installed and has a history and track record vastly better known and more impressive than that of the company or product itself. For example, Steve Jobs, Lee Iacocca, Ross Perot, and Donald Trump have become names of greater significance than the enterprises they manage. As such, their presence in press releases or publicity efforts—the extent to which the messages might be about them—should be specifically defined relative to the product or company.

An *event tied to your product or company* is just that. The focus remains on the *event,* with the product or company identified only as the generous benefactor.

Another first step is to be clear about the objective of your publicity effort. Presenting a message to the public can be a fairly mechanical process, but what exactly do you want to have your publicity accomplish? A quick response might be "to sell the product" or "to make the subject better known." The first answer is wrong in that even the most successful publicity campaign doesn't *sell* more than perhaps an idea. The second answer is legitimate but fairly broad—rather like a shotgun statement. Consider which entries on this list might be among your product, company, service, business, cause, event, association, or campaign objectives:

- inform
- educate
- entertain
- motivate
- inspire
- create awareness
- increase awareness
- increase level of interest
- create an image
- change an image
- alter public perceptions
- increase traffic
- develop a mailing list
- build a database
- support fund-raising efforts
- increase market share
- build brand loyalty
- respond to critics
- avert special-interest-group protests
- encourage volunteerism
- build a volunteer organization

The other first is to determine your audience: *To whom is the message of your campaign directed?*

Whether you describe it as your audience, your public, or your market, the most efficient approach is to aim your particular message at a specific target, which may include:

- media
- customers
- prospects
- shareholders

- members
- securities analysts
- regulators, legislators
- your own trade, profession, or industry
- demographically defined segments, such as:
    men or women of specific ages or regions
    seniors (the "mature" market)
    baby boomers
    parents
    students
    specific ethnic communities
    the gay community
- audiences defined by special interests, such as:
    sports fans
    music lovers
    environmentalists
    travelers
    hunters/sports enthusiasts
    gardeners
    smokers
    observers of politics/public interests
    hobbyists

The list can be as long and specific as your needs demand; certainly no campaign need be limited to any single target audience.

The point of focusing first on the *firsts,* then, is to help identify the following:

- Who or what is the subject of your message?
- What is the objective of your publicity plan?
- To whom is your message directed?

What makes the subject outstanding or unique? Avoid answering with terms such as *good, better,* and *best,* which are self-serving and subjective labels and to which the public has largely become immune—at least when it comes to promotional messages. Is there a product offered that is not touted by its producer as the best? Try asking the respective chairpersons of Coke and Pepsi which product tastes *better.*

Consider too that for the members of your target audience, the primary concern is how the subject of your message affects *them.* The fact that you are number one is lovely for you, but is it a reason enough for others to care? Don't assume it is.

An important aspect of planning and a good way to help define the value of your subject to your public is to ask questions such as:

- What aspects of the product are most important to the customer?
- What fact about the upcoming event is important to the audience?
- What is it the candidate is going to do that is of the greatest concern to the voters?

In social encounters, polite folks may often start out by saying, "So, tell me something about yourself," but what they really want to know is, "What is it about you that I will be interested in knowing for how it affects me?"

The publicist's challenge is not only to get the message out to the target audience, but also to establish a personal connection between the message and the target audience: why they should care and feel a desire to respond.

AT A GLANCE
PUBLICITY: DEFINITIONS AND DISTINCTIONS

- Publicity is about publicizing a subject, creating attention, getting noticed.

- *Bad* publicity is easier to get and more difficult to undo and will, more often than not, have a more lasting impact than the good news.

- Publicity is often thought to be the same as press agentry, promotions, and public relations. This is not the case. Each is a different, if sometimes overlapping, discipline.

- The advantages of advertising include the ability to control content, timing, and frequency of your message; disadvantages are the high cost and lessening of credibility resulting from the fact that the audience knows the message was paid for.

- The old rules of public civility appear to have been broadened to permit frontal attacks on competitors and critics, including calling their ethics into question.

- If attacked, be prepared to respond. If you attack first, be prepared to have your fire returned, and anticipate what the other party's response will be. Determine how far you want to go.

- Some media companies do give favored editorial treatment to advertisers, but don't count on it.

continued

- In order to be consistently effective, a publicist must have the eye, ear, goodwill, and current phone numbers of the proper media people to help present the message to the public.

- A publicist is most effective when the focus is on the subject, not the publicist.

- When publicity is only one part of a larger public relations or marketing plan, a lack of coordination can short-circuit its effectiveness.

- Information is a publicist's essential tool.

- A publicist cannot effectively disseminate or manage information if he or she does not *have* the information. Companies and clients need to provide the necessary information to accomplish the objective.

- Planning provides the road map to the publicity effort's success. Have a plan.

- The public wants to know how the subject of your message will affect them. A publicist's job is to tell them.

2

Form and Substance

THE RULES OF PUBLICITY

Publicists know that word of mouth—that most revered means of communication after all these years—carries the added impact of intimate personal communication, though it tends to reach significantly fewer people than a minute on *Oprah Winfrey*.

The politician racing around, shaking hands at the factory gate, shopping mall, commuter station, and college campus, may reach several hundred people with his or her message in a single 14-hour day—and another million or more people in a 15-second "sound bite" on the evening news.

The Lincoln-Douglas debates are referenced in virtually all U.S. history books and are held to be an event of singular importance in American politics. The number of people who actually saw or heard the debates is less than the number of people who sit through the commercials on reruns of *Cheers* on any given evening. Lincoln and Douglas didn't have TV.

But Kennedy and Nixon did. The first Kennedy-Nixon debate, some 100 years later, is said to represent the day television decided an American election. The audience was substantial, though it was still smaller than the audience for *The Today Show*.

Without a doubt, the media is the message, and not incidentally, the media is the most effective way of communicating the message, whether the substance has to do with politics, the environment, an arts festival, or the appearance for the very first time of a plastic Christmas tree that sings holiday songs, showcased on all the local and network news shows . . . and available at fine stores everywhere. The power of a product on television cannot be overstated. News anchors, talk show hosts, or reporters idly mentioning products from Cabbage Patch dolls and Beanie Babies to oat bran muffins have been known to deplete retailers' stock across the country in a day.

Once again, it must be noted that advertising affords a means of controlling the time and space to present a message soberly or patriotically, sentimentally, with the roar of an enthusiastic, well-rehearsed crowd, with humor or with song—but for a price.

And the size of the audience (the prize) determines the size of the price. Advertisers have paid a half million dollars to have their spot run on TV's hit comedy series *Seinfeld;* a 30-second commercial on the annual Super Bowl in 1998 cost $1.3 million, or $43,333 per second. Local and cable channels are typically well below network, but again, if the program delivers the audience, the rates will reflect it.

Another drawback is ad clutter, which drives people nuts, as too many commercials interrupt favorite programs too often.

Since the Federal Communications Commission in the 1980s eliminated any controls on the number of commercials a broadcast or cable channel could run during a given hour, the average TV program is interrupted every *few minutes* for several minutes of ads. Yet, people continue to watch and, despite their complaints, and in large numbers, buy the products advertised much to their annoyance.

In between the commercials are something called programs, and here's where the opportunities for the publicist come in.

For years, many advertisers would choose print, radio, or outdoor space because to buy time on television, despite its enormous reach and power, was expensive to the point of being prohibitive. But, when it came to television, publicity had its own problems. In many respects, TV was a snob medium, choosing to present only certain stories, subjects, companies, or people it deemed to be highly "visual" enough to be worthy of consideration.

In order to get on TV, the theory insisted, the story had to be big—much bigger than the types of things newspapers or radio would run. TV demanded stories with action, movement, and drama. Today's programming featuring hours of "talking-head" interviews or stories about, for example, business, finance, or research was unheard of just a short time ago.

All that has changed. The visual medium learned that audiences found a close-up of a nervous executive perspiring under television's hot lights and *60 Minutes'* hot questioning to be good theater and every bit as exciting as a car chase. Authors as experts, pitching books on the broadest possible range of subjects, from aviation to zoology; social activists, health experts, and environmentalists pitching warnings; and farmers examining crops at close range proved to hold an audience's attention in early morning, during late night, and in-between.

The expanding number of television channels, both UHF broadcast and cable, has created a need for programming beyond the traditional fare of movies and off-network series reruns. Additionally, programmers find that news shows, TV "magazine" programs, and talk shows not only attract loyal audiences but also are among the least expensive programs to produce. Cable channels in particular have created "niche" networks covering various areas of special interest (ESPN and CNN/SI for sports; CNN, Headline News, and Fox News for news and features; CNBC and MSNBC for talk, call-in, and features; MTV and VH1 for music, film, and fashion-industry news features; Lifetime "Television for Women"; and more). Virtually all of these and other "networks" use on-screen guests for feature segments and interviews, as well as promotion-oriented material on issues, causes, products, and opinions. The Travel Channel, The Weather Channel, Arts & Entertainment, The Discovery Channel—all represent an expanding list of opportunities for publicity.

Many clients, companies, associations, candidates, causes, charities, and people can't afford to advertise even if they wanted to. Of course, many don't want to, recognizing that an interview or a mention on a news or talk show not only comes without the substantial cost of advertising but also carries the additional credibility and often a seemingly implied endorsement that results from being part of the "program content."

It is not unusual to hear an advertising program or a public relations campaign dismissed as:

- all style and no substance
- the sizzle without the steak
- perception versus reality

Now that these major clichés have been dispensed with, the actual matter of form, style, and substance can be addressed. The style can be added later, but substance cannot.

Take the directive to "build a program" literally, and recognize that any building must be done on a solid base: substance. That typically means information.

Sometimes all the necessary information is readily available, but sometimes it takes research to collect it. Research studies and surveys can be expensive, but the information that results from the effort is often critical to the success of the publicity program. How much the publicist knows about the subject, its history, and the principal participants is important.

Before taking your message out to your audience, it is also worth knowing how your subject is perceived by your audience—specifically with regard to your own product, company, or people, as well as relative to others in your industry, category, or profession.

If you are seeking to publicize a fund-raising event: how have similar events been received in your area? Are you presenting a lecture series without having determined whether or not there is an interest level to support it? A classical music concert? A rock concert? An auction? A carnival? Advance research can save effort, money, and time, not to mention averting the problems that come from a failed program if the data suggest that your target group is not likely to support such a program.

• A brokerage firm was disappointed at the low turnout for what it promised would be an excellent seminar on a very timely subject. Fewer than 400 people came to a presentation that was hoping for 1,200. Some advance research would have told the planners that several similar programs had been presented during the year, and the market had, in effect, been saturated. Knowing this in advance could have prompted the planners to change the location, delay their program until more distance was put between it and the last preceding program, or simply change their publicity strategy to emphasize how their program was uniquely different from the others.

• A local PTA had similarly scheduled a dinner-dance, hoping to raise money for its school. The event was poorly attended, not because it wasn't a lovely affair and well planned, but because the people of the school district had been asked to attend so many other functions that year that most simply believed they didn't have the time to give. A bit of advance research would have saved the embarrassment to the PTA of a poorly attended function, saved the effort and expense of putting the event together, and found that the people being targeted for participation in the fund-raiser would have willingly written a check that would have raised the amount that was the goal of the event.

These are simple examples, but each underscores the importance of the type of data that research can provide.

Get the Information

Publicity programs are not fingerprints, of which it is said no two are alike. It is not only possible but also very appropriate for a successful publicity campaign to be adapted to another product, company, service, issue, cause, or individual. The basic rules of what to do and how to do it will likely remain unchanged:

> Do your homework.
> Know your subject.
> Know your market.
> Know whom you are talking to.
> Know what you want to say.
> Know what you want to accomplish.
> Know how much time you have to do it.
> Know how much money you have to spend.
> Be professional.
> Always rewind the tape before returning it.

What is most likely *not* the same in every situation is the subject, product, or issue—even within the same company or organization. For this reason, gathering data—collecting the most complete and up-to-date information—is the rule that must be applied before any of the other rules listed here can be followed.

Even before the publicity effort is outlined, publicists for a sporting event, an auto show, an art exhibition, a press conference, a science fair, a rodeo, or any other event each need to know:

- what else is going on at the same time
- the level of interest in the subject by the audience being targeted for participation
- if anything of a similar nature has been done in the recent past—or ever—and with what result
- how the audience feels about what you have to offer relative to what is being offered or promised elsewhere
- anything else about the subject that may be useful or helpful

A short-cut to commissioning studies and surveys is to look at what your counterparts, competitors, and rivals have been doing, based on how it has been publicized, and evaluate how successful it has been for them. You may then consider adapting a successful formula, customized to reflect your own subject's uniqueness, for your use, or learning from the mistakes of others and going in another direction—applying the questions relating to attitudes and perceptions to that direction as well.

Two forms of research to avoid are the highly unscientific and unreliable "trend shops" which came into fashion in the 1980s and that use research principles similar to those of a crystal ball, and what is commonly called "mother-in-law" research (with apologies to mothers-in-law everywhere) because it basically says, "Let's try it this way because my mother-in-law and everyone in her garden club like it." Sexism aside, similar opinions of everyone in your father-in-law's poker game should be disallowed. The point is that reasonably reliable research is a responsible and worthwhile investment in creating an effective plan.

The *form* in which the information comes to the publicist is less important. It can be a written history, a file of annual reports, volumes of old press clippings, newsletters, or facts accumulated from interviews. What is important is that the information comes together.

Where form becomes relevant is in the final presentation of the material for review by the object of the publicity plan: the media and the public or other target audience. Different media entities have different requirements as to how they will accept material.

A WORD ABOUT COSTS

Very often a public relations program with an emphasis on publicity will be chosen over an advertising plan largely due to costs. It is not uncommon to hear the comment "We expect to get a million dollars worth of *free publicity.*"

Such things have happened, but not often enough to be expected consistently. While the idea of having your message appear wherever, whenever, and however you want it has tremendous appeal—and creative, well-executed ads and commercials are certainly memorable—it is also a very pricey proposition. The operative words in the previous sentence are *ads* and *commercials,* those being the means by which to guarantee a fully controlled message being presented. The best vehicles to carry the ad messages are run by people who know what they've got and charge for it accordingly.

But a publicity campaign is not an advertising campaign. Besides the added credibility of a publicity-driven story's appearing in the media (and the public's accepting that your message is so worthwhile that you don't have to pay to have it carried), there is in fact a typically lower cost to PR than advertising.

But "lower cost" does not mean "free." Many companies, service groups, and trade associations that have a PR agency or consultant on retainer for amounts in the area of $20,000 per month or more may spend less than that on trade or community advertising. There are also the costs of media kits, photos, literature, premiums, banners, and other related expenses to be considered.

A typical guideline is: the larger the client or subject, and the higher the stakes, the higher the fee. Tobacco companies, furriers, and the pharmaceutical industry, for example, recognize the importance publicity has on their particular constituencies, and each spends and invests a considerable amount annually in employing publicists to get their message out.

It may be *cheaper,* but it is definitely not *cheap.*

WHO'S IN CHARGE HERE?

President John F. Kennedy was fond of noting that "victory has a hundred fathers and defeat is an orphan." Obviously he was suggesting that when a job goes well, people who want to take credit for it are easy to find. However, when an effort falls apart, no one wants to take responsibility. Nearly four decades after President Kennedy made that observation, it is fair to say that things have not changed at all.

In some companies, firms, associations, and other types of organizations, it is not uncommon to find:

The Publicity Committee
Vice President of Marketing
Vice President of Public Relations
Director of Communications
Public Relations Manager
Investor Relations Manager
Media Relations Manager
Joe the doughnut guy

. . . all wanting to have some say in how the publicity effort is run, all quick to point out what they believe is lacking, and all perfectly willing to be out of town and to not return phone calls when something goes wrong.

In the best of all possible worlds, one person will have responsibility for carrying out the day-to-day tactics of the publicity plan, will call on resources within the organization as needed, and will have the confidence of the media to do the job effectively.

If, however, corporate politics are a significant part of your way of life—also not uncommon, particularly in an organization in which a significant number of "volunteers" are involved and, as such, must be shown a degree of deference—a two-stage approach may be useful.

STAGE I

- Everyone involved (committees, officers, directors, managers) should be invited to a "brainstorming" session quarterly to hear a current situation analysis and to contribute their ideas.
- One person must be designated as the everyday point person and media contact.

- At the meetings, have an agenda; control the meeting (an old expression is: He who controls the agenda controls the meeting).
- Solicit ideas.
- Develop the good ideas (and give credit where credit is due).
- Tell the contributors who advanced *bad* ideas that the suggestions are under consideration, write them down, put them in a drawer, and never look at them again.
- Use the good ideas to help develop a strategy outline.

STAGE II

- Clearly define your objectives.
- Identify your target audience; this will determine who and what names belong on your main media list.
- Develop the media list.
- Develop the press kit.
- Develop a schedule.
- Get to work.

Standard Rate and Data Corporation has for years published the definitive set of directories for advertising and public relations media information. Other directories from the Public Relations Society of America (PRSA) and various local publicity clubs, as well as Bacon's are also useful tools.

THE TOOLS OF PUBLICITY

As noted, the essential element of a successful publicity effort is *the plan*. Without it, people have a way of remembering assignments differently and/or too easily being diverted or distracted by events and comments along the way. Too often, something as simple as a reference in the press to a CEO's "misguided strategy" can cause a CEO to *alter* that strategy, sometimes without telling his or her own people. The resulting confusion and miscues can be amusing to watch—unless you're a part of the company, a stock-holder, or a member of the CEO's team. Effective communication to a target audience will likely miss the target if internal communication is not effective as well. The same rule applies if the subject is a school, a hospital, an association, a practice, a special-interest group, and so forth.

The plan should be written and should include the:

- objectives
- strategies to achieve the objectives
- tactics
- budget
- time frame in which the objectives are to be achieved

This list can be developed by a group sitting around a table in an office or conference room, but at some point people are going to have to leave that room and set about making the plan work. At that point they should be armed with the very basic tools of a publicity effort, whether it is for a one-time event or an ongoing program.

WHAT A PUBLICIST SHOULD KNOW

A publicist should know his or her client and subject very well, the appropriate media to contact with the subject message, basic skills of the art or science of communication, and how not to get lost in New York when meeting a reporter who is on a tight deadline. There are also some essential terms with which the publicist should be familiar. The following list is not, by any means, a complete glossary, but a fairly basic guide to terms that are frequently misunderstood.

[**ADI**] area of dominant influence; a research term that basically tells which media entity has the largest audience share

[**advertorial**] the print version of the infomercial; an ad written and designed to resemble a newspaper editorial or news story; thought by some to be a deceptive approach, although it doesn't have to be, as Mobil Oil Corporation, for one, has demonstrated over some three decades of using the form effectively

[**background**] information provided to the media with the understanding that it will clarify a subject without identifying the source of the information

[**backgrounder**] a document that incorporates history, biographical information, and fact-sheet data into a concise overview; a profile; a briefing document that provides the media with a quick take on its subject

[**dateline**] the point of origin and date of record shown on press releases and news stories

[**deep background**] a promise from the media to protect the identity of a source in exchange for the source's providing information that is frequently considered to be of a highly sensitive and confidential nature

[**demographics**] a research term that segments an audience or market by characteristics such as age, sex, income, occupation, ethnicity, or geographical area

[**media alert**] an advance notice sent to news services and newswires, indicating that a major announcement is forthcoming; an advisory or comment on an item of interest

[**media tour**] scheduled on-site interviews with media entities in a designated area over a specified time period

[**no comment**] a standard phrase indicating a refusal of someone to provide information; it invariably looks to the media and the world as if the person is guilty of some wrongdoing or is hiding something; a more advisable response that achieves the same purpose: "It would be inappropriate to comment on that matter at this time, but I would be pleased to provide information as it becomes appropriate."

[**off the record**] information provided to the media with the understanding that it will not be referenced in a story and is provided only in response to inquiries to help further the reporter's understanding of the subject; another term for trouble (the publicist's best rule here is "If you don't want to see it in the story, don't say it.")

[**press kit**] media kit; an envelope, folder, or packet of material containing essential information such as bios, photos, fact sheets, reprints of published articles, press releases, brochures, and tapes

[**press release**] a document prepared for, and disseminated to, the media to announce or address a specific subject

[**sound bite**] a short, quotable remark; it is often heavy in color and impact, while light on substance

[**spin**] to shift the focus of a subject; to influence or interpret a story in a way favorable to a particular point of view

[**target**] the specific segment of the total market to be the focus of the publicity effort

[**USP**] unique selling point (or proposition or principle) that is a subject's point of differentiation

[**VNR**] video news release; typically a 55-second to 120-second video version of a press release—not a commercial, but an informational presentation on a specific subject focusing on who, what, when, where, why, and how

To be most effective, a publicist should learn "the language of" the industry in which the message is based and to which it is directed. This is appropriate for two reasons: first, to be as informed as possible in the particular subject area in which the publicist is working, and second, to be in a position to explain, clarify, or "translate," if necessary, very industry-specific terms and information to the publicist's media constituency or to the public. It is not uncommon for a fact sheet, a spec sheet, or other industry documents to be heavy in "trade jargon." One of the publicist's functions is to simplify and explain such information as may be necessary.

THE PRESS KIT

The press kit is to the publicist what a money bag is to the guard in the armored car: you can carry the stuff around without it, but it certainly is useful to keep everything together where and as it should be. Also sometimes referred to as a *media kit* or *media package,* under normal circumstances when the subject might be a product, a company, an event, an association, a service organization, an issue, a candidate, or a cause, it should contain:

- the name, phone number, and E-mail number of a contact person, including an "after-hours" number
- a press release summarizing the subject in 500 words or less
- a fact sheet and/or backgrounder giving the history and a "context" for the subject
- at least one photograph of the person, people, or product(s) representing the subject of the publicity effort
- any relevant speech transcripts or copies of press clippings that provide color and texture to the subject
- any relevant product spec sheets, company annual reports, or brochures that offer additional information on the subject

- in certain situations, a videotape, a compact disc,
  an audiotape, or a book on the subject, if relevant,
  supporting the message as outlined in the printed material
- anything else that might be of particular interest either to
  the entire media list or to a particular recipient of a kit

Despite the growing trend toward electronic communication, the press kit is still the cornerstone and all-around utility piece of the typical publicity effort. It is the press kit that is typically kept in the reporter's, editor's or producer's file, often for an indefinite period. Even high-tech products and companies, while including a disc in the kit, still must develop a traditional press kit as outlined here, because that is the standard acceptable form in which the media receive material.

Will this ever change? Possibly, but for a large segment of the media, this form will remain *the* form. Having duly noted that, for those reporters and editors who wish to use electronic communication as their main mode, the basic press kit should be available in E-mail form, as well as in hard copy form, and if appropriate to the subject, a website should be created to provide a file with as much information on the subject as is appropriate, basically an adaptation of material in the press kit as outlined.

Photographs

Some publicists put a great emphasis on the importance of photographs, both in the press kit and outside of it. The reasons for this are numerous:

- The expression "A picture is worth a thousand words"
  may be old and threadbare, but it is still true. Many
  people—members of the media included—form opinions
  from looking at pictures that they can't always get from
  reading a press release or fact sheet. To that end, if the

"essence" of the story, message, or product can be
"suggested" by a photograph and a well-written caption,
the publicist is ahead of the game.

- Sometimes even the most well-intentioned writers, editors,
  and producers do not read or review everything included
  in a press kit—and it is a great mistake for publicists to
  assume that they do. A photograph with a well-written
  caption can often convey the basic message that the rest
  of the material explains in detail.
- Newspaper and magazine stories that include photographs
  receive more attention and score higher on recall tests.
- Visual material very often provokes an immediate and
  emotional response. A text or narrative can be loaded with
  statistics, facts, and pages of descriptive adjectives that
  leave the reviewer cold, but a well-done photograph of a
  product or person in a complementary setting can evoke
  very positive reactions. A person can seem serious,
  businesslike, friendly, youthful, mature, alert, confident,
  eccentric, or any of a longer list of characteristics by virtue
  of his or her appearance in a photograph. If two posters
  are side by side, and one has a photograph, the other only
  text, the photo-poster is far more likely to be remembered
  and to influence how the viewer feels about the subject.
- Research indicates that people trust what they *see*. Charles
  Schwab, founder of the giant discount brokerage firm that
  bears his name, reportedly told a business associate that
  his smartest move was putting his name on the door and
  his picture in the ads because people like to see the person
  who is taking their money.
- People like to look at pictures.

Having laid out an argument *for* photographs to help generate publicity, it should be noted that some publicists go overboard
by including too many photos in press kits or with press releases,

or they stage or contrive a pose or scene that diminishes the subject rather than enhances it. In publicity, with photographs as with everything else, leave the audience (both the public and your media audience) wanting to see more.

Black-and-white photos either 5" × 7" or 8" × 10" (no larger) are the media's choice.

How many photos should go into a press kit? There is no one right response to that. The answer is: only the number necessary to support the point of the subject.

Without a press kit, one photo should accompany a press release whenever possible. It may be a photograph of an individual who is either the subject of, or quoted in, the press release. In these situations a "working candid" photo makes the best impression, as opposed to a posed, studio portrait. Remember that newspapers and magazines want to convey a sense of *what's going on* to their readers, and a studio portrait is not going on. A photograph of a person at a desk with a facial expression that suggests conversation, activity, movement, reaction, thoughtfulness, or another mood or emotion is more effective than a stiff, forced smile.

Avoid cliché photographs with telephones or sheets of noticeably blank paper to suggest action.

Within a press kit, the ideal number of photographs is related to the subject of the material. A photograph of a person quoted in a release is appropriate. If the subject is a product, a product photo is obviously in order. Whenever possible, people should be in the photographs to offer perspective (size, distance) and because showing people interacting with products or objects is usually more visually interesting than the objects alone.

The media are also more responsive to (and more inclined to use) photographs that include people.

Captions to photographs should be more than mere identifiers. They should be, essentially, capsule versions of the subject or story:

Weak   Mrs. B. P. Fizzwater and her daughter Lucy.

Better   Mrs. B. P. Fizzwater (left) and her daughter
                Lucy Ann Fizzwater dedicate the $6.7
                million meditation garden honoring the
                late philanthropist Buster P. Fizzwater.
                The two-square-acre garden is in suburban
                Humtown, Ohio, where Mr. Fizzwater once
                served briefly as a justice of the peace.

In press kits used to publicize a seminar or an exhibition, individual photographs of all speakers should be included with copies
of their bios. In press kits to be used for business or corporate promotion, a single photo of the founder is OK, but if, for example,
the company or firm had four founding partners, a group photo of
the four is better than four individual photos, in the interests of
space in the kit as well as space in the publication, and to minimize
the chance of persons being misidentified.

Some publications, upon agreeing to do the publicist's story,
will send out their own photographer to have an original exclusive
photo to accompany the story. In such cases consider taking photos
at the same time, and if your photos prove to be more flattering to
the subject, press and beg to have your photos (offered exclusively)
used as an alternative to the less flattering one(s). In any event, a
publicist can always make use of a flattering photo in a brochure,
poster, speech, or program listing or in any number of other ways.

The cost of good photography is often misunderstood. Perhaps
it has to do with the fact that so many weekend "amateur photographers" with fine, relatively expensive cameras have taken some very
good photos of fishing trips, vacations, and the kids' school play that
there is a feeling that a candid shot or two or three of the boss or the
client, sitting at a desk or conference table, or making a speech,
shouldn't cost very much. Well, sometimes it does, and it should.

Given the importance of very good photography—and the
possibility that it will indeed drive the press release across the editor's desk and result in a far better placement than material arriv-
ing without photos—the cost is *especially* worth it.

It is common for newspaper photographers to "moonlight"
and to take additional photos on their own time. Their rates are
usually quite fair. Local publicity groups and public relations clubs
and societies can often recommend freelance photographers who
are competent, professional, and affordable and who understand
how the photos will be used.

Explain the assignment to the photographer, and share the
objective of the campaign, so there is no misunderstanding about
what needs to be done. Agree on a fee, and pay your bills promptly.
As competitive as writers and photographers are, the community is
a close one where people talk, and clients who don't pay their bills
quickly receive the kind of publicity in "the business" that is not
good for anyone's business.

THE PRESS RELEASE

The press release is the calling card of the publicist. It is basically
the essence of the message the publicist wants to present. It is very
often the first thing the writer, reporter, or editor looks for in a
press kit and the first item to be requested if it is not immediately
visible. Much as some people are judged by others' first impression, the press release is often regarded as the first impression of a
campaign to follow or of an image to be defined.

Press releases should be written in form and tone as if they
were the actual stories as they might appear in a newspaper or magazine or as they might be read on the news. While most publications
will not print the press release exactly as it is presented to them, pre-
ferring to have a staff writer reinterpret the material in the publication's own style, the press release should nonetheless be of such a
professional standard that it could very well be used as presented. It
should incorporate the basic elements of a well-crafted news story,
telling who, what, when, where, why, and how. Reporters and editors especially love press releases that emphasize names, dates, dollars, and other definitive factual points.

First, consider form and the *look* of the press release. Determine on what letterhead or masthead the release is to be printed: Is it that of the originating company or client? A PR agency? A letterhead with a graphic specifically created for this announcement or campaign? Plain paper?

Keep in mind that many editors or reporters will request that releases be faxed to them, and that a very detailed or "busy" graphic can close up or fill in when faxed and end up at the receiving end looking like a thumbprint or a coffee stain. If you're using a graphic on your press release (or on your regular letterhead), consider that the quality of machines sending and receiving copies will vary— and so will the impression the publicist or company will make.

This simple determination about the look of the paper selected is important in the way that it relates to the overall strategy and the impression that is to be created.

Even in the high-tech, futuristic culture of instant communication, the standard format for a press release provides that it:

- is on 8½" × 11" paper
- is typed double-spaced (about 250 words per page)
- lists the name and phone number of at least one contact for further information (two is better), with an after-hours phone number for late calls if necessary
- notes a release date for the material (typically press releases are marked "For immediate release")
- notes a "dateline" (date and point of origin)
- carries a headline that succinctly conveys the subject of the release
- represents the facts and details of the subject in their order of importance, with supporting data, including, as appropriate, quotes from relevant persons connected with the subject

It is not unusual for the originator of a press release, whether a publicist or not, to think that the release is a good opportunity to score some points for creativity and imagination, as well as to stand out from the crowd. Thus, press releases have been distributed that were written on chalkboards, in childlike scrawl, on cans and boxes, on T-shirts, on long rolls of paper resembling scrolls or toilet tissue, and even by singing messengers.

As a rule, the recipients hate this. Try putting a roll of toilet paper or a singing messenger in your file cabinet. While the creative energy employed might not go unnoticed, after the smile or the chuckle, there is the practical aspect to consider. A publicist is a purveyor of information, not the opening act at The Comedy Store.

There is also the temptation to be totally contemporary and use E-mail for press releases. That's fine, just as long as the publicist also uses the traditional form—unless, of course, everyone on the media list has advised the publicist to do otherwise.

Press releases are not ads, histories, or short stories and should not be presented as if they were. Keep it factual, and save the color for the media to add later.

Paragraphs should be short, and the use of exclamation points is discouraged. While this rule is not etched in stone, the ideal press release is no more than two pages (500 words). Although going on to a third page is not the worst of sins, consider whether such additional information (beyond two pages) can and should be in an accompanying "backgrounder" or fact sheet, strictly limiting the release itself to the most concise presentation of information.

Unless the subject of the release has truly world-shaking implications, remember the rule that sometimes "less is more." Editors, writers, and producers, while not wanting to admit it, are more inclined to read short, concise press releases and to take a pass on the longer, more detailed pieces. The more people the release gets re-routed to, the less likely it is to ever resurface and appear in print or on TV.

Respect the media's time and space. Remember that there are many people trying to get the attention of the most desirable media entities and that competition among publicists can be intense. Just as a publicist needs to make the point quickly and succinctly in an oral pitch, reading a press release should not be a time-consuming process.

Consider the content of the release carefully, before labeling it. That is, if the release has no clear news value, do not designate it as a "news release." It can be labeled a "press release" or an "information circular" or simply "information on _____ from _____." Most editors, reporters, and writers have an understanding of what constitutes "news" and will develop a greater respect for a publicist who exercises similar judgment.

Having covered the mechanical requirements for the press release, here are additional requirements that run more to the professionalism of the publicist, serve to increase the prospects of the release being used, and contribute to creating an overall more favorable impression of the subject and its presenter:

- Don't oversell; keep the content factual.
- Be honest. Your critics and competitors are likely to be called to comment on a story you have started in motion. Don't become an easy target for them to criticize or dismiss.
- Know and respect deadlines. To call or send material at or close to production time creates a poor impression of the professionalism of both the publicist and his or her client, company, or cause.
- Be at the phone to take calls following dissemination of a release. The reasons for this should be obvious. To not be available can create an impression that the author of the press release does not *want* to take follow-up calls. There is virtually no upside to creating that impression.

Most everyone at some point blusters about having too much to do and not enough time, often expressing resentment over frequent interruptions and intrusions—even though it may be all part of the job. Reporters, editors, and producers feel the same way. Show the same respect for their time that you would want people to have for your own.

THE BACKGROUNDER

A backgrounder is a briefing document that a publicist prepares for the media, for inclusion in a press kit or to be provided to the press before an interview in order to help the interviewer become more familiar with the subject. It can be as long or as short as it needs to be to convey enough information to help a reporter understand the subject. The document, as the name implies, provides background information, such as history, organization, and high points.

FILLING OUT THE REST OF THE PRESS KIT

The essential elements of the press kit are the *press release, photograph(s),* and a *backgrounder.* What to include beyond that should be determined by referring to the plan's objectives and strategy. If applicable, a research study or survey may support the message the publicist is trying to make. Perhaps, if the research study is of considerable length (more than 50 pages, for example), an "executive summary" of the study (six pages or so) would serve the same purpose and receive more attention, with the full study available upon request.

If the subject of the publicity effort is a corporation, it is common to include a copy of the corporation's current annual report, interim financial reports, and securities analysts' recommendations.

If applicable, profiles or bios (with photographs) of key executives may be included in the press kit, but the operative term is "applicable." The executives must have some relevance to the subject that is the focus of the publicity effort, or the inclusion of executive bios and photos will appear to be a vanity exercise and could even diminish the impact of the material.

Videos, audiotapes, CDs, product samples, and promotional merchandise bearing the subject logo or signature, again, if applicable to the furtherance of the publicity message, may be included *with* the press kit—but not *within* the press kit, where the items' size and shape may distract from the release and the subject's focus material. Without seeing a clear connection to the subject, reporters, editors, and producers tend to relegate the "merchandise" to the "trash and trinkets" category.

The Media List—and What Goes with It

The term *media list* may be self-explanatory, but how a media list is created and how it is used to maximize effectiveness are the more important concerns, and that is where the objectives and strategy portions of the plan must be consulted.

The old adage that when it comes to direct mail, the list is everything has certainly been validated time and again. But in mounting a successful media-relations effort, the media list is only a part of the process—a very important part, to be sure, but still just a part.

If the objective of the plan is, for example, to become better known *within a particular trade, industry, or profession,* to become better identified as a player or a force in the industry, the approach might involve:

- setting up a booth at the major trade shows
- generating a series of press releases in rapid order (such as, perhaps, six releases over a six-month period) to appear in each issue of the monthly trade publications
- creating a steady feed of announcements to daily and weekly trade papers and newsletters
- introducing a new piece of useful—as opposed to strictly promotional—literature (a product brochure, an industry research document such as a survey or a white paper)
- mailing point-of-view letters to target industry centers of influence, such as the trade press, union leaders and members, trade association officers and members, suppliers, and publications that serve suppliers
- arranging for a speech to be delivered by your CEO or another spokesperson
- releasing highlights of a speech to the trade press

The gross result should be that a large percentage of the trade audience—and especially the trade media—has been exposed to your name and presence/participation in industry matters with a regularity over a concentrated period of time. The net result should be to have created a sense within the industry that *these guys are everywhere, so they must be important to our industry or our business.*

The media list in this case is strictly limited to the trade press. If your objective is greater awareness within your industry, there's no need for CNN or *Time* magazine. If your target audience is the electronics industry, then your media list is the electronics trade publications, including a presence in the special publications created for meetings, conventions, and trade shows. If your target audience is the airline industry, ditto the preceding. An exception to this "limit yourself to the trades" rule is a case in which the most influential media in your industry are *outside* of your industry.

For example, a bank wanting to raise its awareness level within the banking industry would certainly focus on bank trade publications and direct mail to an industry list. But since the *Wall Street Journal* is by far the most influential publication read by bankers (as well as by writers and editors in the banking industry trade press), it must be a high priority on the media list in the publicity effort. Other print media, such as the *Financial Times, Business Week, Forbes,* and *Fortune,* as well as CNBC cable television's Financial News Network, are followed by members of the banking industry and influence them, while not being banking media per se.

An exception to the exception is when your bank is the Second National Bank of Grasse Butte, North Dakota (or is it *South Dakota . . .*) and the *Wall Street Journal* is unlikely to devote its coveted national space to covering your story, nor would it likely serve your interests or enhance your position within the industry to be represented there. What then? The answer is back to focusing on the trade press, which *will* profile local or regional subjects of note. Creatively developing a list of matters "of note" for the trades to cover is an illustration of how defining who you are and what you want to say is at least as important as developing the media list.

Your plan, outlining your objectives, strategy, and tactics, is your guide to selecting media you will approach with your story.

Is a print schedule consistent with your objectives? If the answer is yes, then what kind of print media belongs on your list: general, trade, specialty, ethnic, or demographically determined (aimed at women, men, older, younger, affluent, professional, etc.)? Should your choice be limited to newspapers, magazines, newsletters, trade journals? What are your available options among the selected category: daily, weekly, monthly?

Does television help you achieve your objectives? If yes, news or public affairs programs? TV magazine shows, interviews, or talk shows? Lifestyle programs (cooking, sports oriented, fine dining)? Broadcast or cable? Local or national? Radio? If so, what types of programs offer the best formats for your message?

What is the audience for the media you are considering? Are these the people you want to reach with your message? Are they customers, potential customers, people who influence other people?

DEVELOPING AND FINE-TUNING THE LIST

If you have done your homework and you know your subject, the base roster of names on your media list will be the obvious media that you already know cover the subject.

As you answer the questions about print, TV, and radio, a profile should be taking shape, suggesting which publications and/or programs offer the best match to your message.

To your base list of obvious media add your wish list—the *media that you think should be carrying your story.*

Consult the directories published by Standard Rate and Data Service or by Bacon's (segmented by media, such as print, TV, radio, cable) and *Editor & Publisher International Yearbook.* Other directories are available at local and business libraries, but these are three of the most respected and relied-upon resources. Within these directories, locate the names of the media on your list. Note the audience of each entry, and confirm that this is in fact the audience you want to reach. If it's not, delete that entry from your list.

Note that the entries you've located in the directories are arranged by industries. Determine if any of the other entries in that section are appropriate or desirable for inclusion on your list. For example, if you are targeting the advertising industry and believe *Advertising Age* is an obvious inclusion on your base list, in the section that you found *Advertising Age*, note the listing of other publications such as *Adweek*, *Brand Week*, *Electronic Media*, and *Marketing & Media*, and consider if any of these entries belongs on your list.

Get and examine copies of the publications on your list to determine the format in which material is presented. Note also if other media are advertising within your selected publications' pages, and consider, since they are targeting the same audience you are interested in reaching, if they belong on your list as well.

Check your local classified telephone directory under the chosen subject. To continue with the advertising example, look under "advertising" in the Yellow Pages or its counterpart in your area. The subject heading may yield names of advertising publications not listed in the directories.

Consult the local chapter of the Public Relations Society of America (PRSA) or publicity club in your area and inquire as to availability of a current directory. Usually if one is available, membership is required to obtain it.

In many successful public relations agencies there is no one media list. Each client—and frequently, each press release for each client—has a list of its own, customized to reflect the interests not only of the company or product, but also of any specific or unique points of reference noted in the release. For example, a financial services company will have its base list of media contacts, and for one particular release, specific media in the mutual fund industry may be added; for another release, rather than mutual fund media, real estate or insurance-related media will be added. Such customization is not unusual, is appropriately thorough, and minimizes the number of likely disinterested parties receiving the material, while maximizing the list of those more narrowly focused media that are more likely to be interested.

Businesses buy *mailing lists* all the time. There are catalogs of lists and databases with millions of names and addresses, cross-referenced, available by zip codes and assorted demographic combinations. But beware of someone wanting to sell you a *media list*. Reaching out to the media with your story or message is a unique kind of selling. It is not like catalog sales or fund-raising. When a publicist contacts a media representative to present a message or story idea, the publicist is asking the media to join in an effort to carry the message forward to a larger audience. That effort becomes a partnership of sorts, and partners are not bought at a rate of dollars-per-thousand. They are chosen carefully, considered carefully for their value, and treated with a unique appreciation and respect.

Once a publicist has narrowed the list to include media entities, it is time to fine-tune the list to include the names of media *people.*

Each entry on the media list should include the name of an actual living person. In point of fact, as people routinely move up, move on, move over, or move out, a media list can become out of date very quickly. Update lists and double-check for accuracy on a frequent basis: four to six times per year is not too often if you are not certain of the person covering a particular beat.

Check that names are spelled correctly. Few things annoy people as much as having someone who is asking them for the courtesy of their attention not take the time to get their names right—and it happens far too often.

Alas, there are times when there is no alternative but to direct the release, press kit, invitation, or announcement to the "assignment editor" or "business editor." In most cases when this is necessary it is because the particular media organization chooses to either rotate the function or not appoint someone permanently to a particular beat.

Know which media use this procedure. The same editor who insists that one or more items be addressed simply to "the editor" may well take offense when information directed to him or her arrives without a personal greeting.

TARGETING YOUR MEDIA

Once a publicist has clearly identified the objective and prepared the appropriate materials (press releases, fact sheets, bios) and disseminated them, it is time for telephone follow-ups. Sometimes the material will have been misdirected or will not have arrived and will have to be re-sent. Learning that a press kit or a release has not been received may seem like a frustrating delay, but it is quite the opposite, in that having learned *anything at all* in a routine follow-up creates an opportunity for conversation and another chance to promote a subject.

And what about the follow-up call that reveals that the material was received? More than likely the editor, writer, or producer will claim to review the material and see about "doing something with it." Again, use the contact as an opportunity to *sell the message*.

A publicist also understands that, since publicity is not paid advertising, there are no guarantees that 100 press releases sent out will result in even a single placement. This is why follow-up calls to "sell" the subject story are often so critical. Perhaps the press release was not clear enough or failed to make its point. Perhaps the USP wasn't directly stated. Perhaps the media list was overly ambitious and needs to be modified.

The follow-up call will not only help sell the story but also serve to update the targeted media list and evaluate its effectiveness. Make certain to emphasize the benefits of the subject to the audience, as that is the single point that editors find hard to resist. It gives the story *value* to the reader.

AT A GLANCE
FORM AND SUBSTANCE

- One-on-one may be more personal, but using the media is the most effective way of communicating a publicist's message.

- Formerly, to get the interest of TV producers, a story had to be visual—more action, movement, and drama. Now "talking heads" will suffice if the story is interesting (although the media still want to show life rather than still life).

- The growth in TV of cable and satellite channels has created a need for more programming. That, in turn, has created more opportunities for publicists, particularly in the form of news, talk shows, and news "magazine" programs.

- It may seem simplistic, but to be truly effective a publicist needs to know all there is to know about a subject, including its people, events, history, and competition.

- The basic rules for publicists: do your homework; know your subject; know your market; know whom you're talking to; know what you want to say; know what you want to accomplish; know how much time you have to do it; know your budget; be professional.

continued

- Publicists for events need to know what else is going on at the same time; the level of interest of the target audience; what similar events have recently taken place; how successful such events were; how the subject is perceived relative to any competitors; anything else that may be useful.

- Track what competitors and rivals do as part of your research (again, getting to know all you can about your subject).

- Avoid using unreliable, unscientific "nonresearch" such as the information provided by "trend shops" and mother-in-law research ("It's true because my family *thinks* it's true").

- A good publicity program may cost less than some other forms of spreading a message (such as advertising), but it should not be assumed to be free. Publicizing can involve printing, promotion, and event charges, as well as fees for service. Less costly, perhaps, but there is rarely if ever truly such a thing as "free" publicity.

- Ideally one person in a company, organization, or publicity campaign will have responsibility for day-to-day operations and for speaking on behalf of the effort. Having more than one spokesperson can confuse and diminish the effectiveness of the effort.

- Develop a strategy outline.

- Clearly define objectives; identify your target audience; develop a media list; develop a press kit; develop a schedule.

continued

- A publicity plan should be written that includes objectives, strategies, tactics, a budget, and a time frame in which the objectives are to be achieved.

- Being creative is a nice idea, but the media have a standard format for press releases. Know it and use it.

- Appreciate the importance of a well-done photograph with a good caption for editors and writers who don't read or review all material provided by a publicist.

- A good press release reads like a good news story, making certain to note who, what, when, where, why, and how.

- Use a letterhead and a press release masthead that will copy and fax clearly: on $8^{1}/_{2}$" × 11" paper, double-spaced, with names and phone numbers of contacts, release date, dateline, a strong headline, and concise copy.

- Try to keep press releases to two pages, using fact sheets and backgrounders to provide more detail.

- In press releases, keep the content factual; be honest. Reporters and editors love press releases that emphasize names, dates, numbers, and other definitive, factual information.

- Know and respect deadlines.

- Be available to take phone calls following issuance of a press release.

- Backgrounders are briefing documents that outline a subject's history, organization, and high points.

- A media list tells whom to contact and why: what objective each entry on the list is to achieve.

- It is likely that there will be more than one media list, depending on what each press release is to accomplish.

3

Different Strokes: Understanding Media

MEDIA "COMPETITION"

You're looking for publicity. You've got a story to tell. In the words of *Ghostbusters,* "Who you gonna call?"

You've got a lot of choices. Depending on your strategy, your list of targeted media may be lengthy and diverse (general-interest print, radio, broadcast TV news), somewhat narrow (a particular industry trade press), or very narrow (exclusive reports in a weekly newsletter, or information disseminated only via the Internet).

To quote Martin Mayer quoting Neil Borden, "Markets make media." Whom we want to talk to, what we want to say to them, and how we want to say it have a lot to do with *where* we want to say it: what media we want to target to help us carry our message. Mayer sees a problem in what he concludes is the existence of too many markets and the fact that they overlap.

He writes, "There are local markets, regional markets, national markets. There are male and female markets. There is an upper-middle-class market, a middle-class market, a lower-class market. There are urban, rural, and (definitely, now; painstaking research has proved the visible fact) suburban markets. There are old-folks markets, middle-aged markets, young-married markets, teenage markets, children's markets. And, of course, there are the markets segregated by common interests: the home-furnishings-and-decorations market, the

57

sports-car market, the high-fidelity market, the fashion market. To reach these many markets, there are many media: some 1,750 daily newspapers, 450 television and 3,300 radio broadcasting stations, 600 consumer magazines . . ."

Mayer was identifying markets and media for an advertising audience, but the point is valid as well for the publicist. The goal is identifying the target audience for your message, identifying the media to which the audience (or audiences) turn for their information, and customizing, packaging, and focusing your message to the audience—your market—and the media in the form that will have the greatest impact.

Sometimes something that is a publicity effort makes news; often news makers use the fact that they are receiving attention by being in the news as an opportunity to generate more publicity.

Are the media always objective?

No, not always. The issue of why this is the case and how it came to pass—and the fact that there may well be people who disagree, and both sides will trot out their research to support their conclusions—is best left for another forum. The point is that this can be used by the publicist to advantage. The publicist must learn the predisposition of various media entities and act accordingly.

The word *scoop* isn't used much in the modern media vernacular (and for that matter, neither is *vernacular*). A "scoop" was once a hot item that pretty much every media outlet wanted, but one reporter, paper, or broadcaster got there first. It was an exclusive piece of information of enough importance that other media would be forced to scramble to catch up, follow up, and gamely attempt to put their own spin on the story.

While "scoops" may be rarer in the age of instantaneous electronic communication, "exclusives" are not. Major media are still as competitive as ever, and which reporter, publication, network, or station gets the "exclusive" interview relating to an important story often becomes as important to the media as the story itself. The 24-hour cable news television stations are intensely competitive and will often boast about who beat the other in getting a story on TV first, if only by minutes.

• The *New York Times* was the first publication to publish the "Pentagon Papers," revealing highly damaging information about United States policy during the Vietnam War. The information was provided to the *Times* "exclusively" by a government employee, and more than three decades later the paper was still referring to its having broken this important story. Had it not been an "exclusive," it would have ranked as merely another story covered. Numerous people connected with the story effectively publicized their participation in it and both profited financially and brought greater attention and clarity to the antiwar movement.

• Billionaire business executive H. Ross Perot announced his presidential candidacy on CNN TV's *Larry King Live* and helped to position the cable network as a major player in breaking news. Many people believe that his announcement would not have had the impact it did, had Perot delivered it on one of the major Sunday-morning network TV news shows. There seemed to be an extra element of news in the maverick candidate's declaring his candidacy on the maverick network.

• The public's fascination with the Watergate story of the early 1970s was fueled by the "exclusive" series of reports in the *Washington Post*. That series made investigative reporting so competitive a practice that publicists, on behalf of their employers and clients, would desperately seek a friendly media entity to whom they might "exclusively" offer their side of the story. Although other media were covering the story at the same time, the intensity and attention to detail—the focused follow-through by the *Post*—gave justification to its reporters' claim of exclusivity of certain sources and information. The *Post,* not incidentally, has heavily publicized its role in the Watergate story over the years as an example of its aggressive journalism. This has greatly helped the paper rise from modest pre-Watergate status to one of the most influential newspapers in the United States.

- On a more local level, the president of the school board was about to resign under pressure. He chose to give his resignation story "exclusively" to a certain newspaper reporter on the day prior to its becoming public knowledge. The reporter's paper gave it front-page treatment and, in doing so, allowed the resigning officer to "control the tone" of the story by putting out his version first and not taking questions from critics until after the agenda had been set by the initial story. Could critics still raise questions? Of course. The newspaper had not compromised itself because it had not promised a favorable story, but had only granted favorable *positioning* in exchange for the exclusive. The president had the "first-strike advantage" in influencing public opinion by leading the story.

Whether the story is corporate, personal, financial, or political—an announcement (or withdrawal) of candidacy, the opening of a clinic, a new-product introduction or a new venture, or the first look at a new program or process—the *New York Times,* the *Wall Street Journal,* CBS, ABC, NBC, CNN, and Fox, as well as the lowest-circulation, small-town daily newspaper will work every source and contact they have in order to be, if not always first with the story, at least there with an *exclusive* version from someone of significance.

Arranging "exclusives" represents an opportunity for publicists to cultivate inside contacts who will logically be receptive to future material the publicist has to offer.

An announcement at a press conference or a statement in a news release, issued so that all interested media receive it at once, is fine for noncontroversial stories. But a good reporter, after receiving a release or an announcement, will go for follow-up questions—often to opponents, rivals, or critics—and the comments that result may be more dramatic or newsworthy than the original statement, thus fully changing the direction of the announcement.

Increasingly, in matters of controversy, protests by special-interest groups, or being the focus of a government action, such as those of the tobacco industry, pharmaceutical industry, or agricultural interests, the publicist's ability to locate and cultivate at least a fair and objective, if not totally sympathetic, media contact can be critical. By offering information, details, or a spokesperson exclusively to a particular media entity, the publicist increases the likelihood of getting "bigger play"—more time, space, promotion, and follow-up—than if the particular media contact were only one of many to get the story at the same time.

Understanding the prominence, effectiveness, and strength of each media entity is important, but understanding the competitive nature of media and cultivating media contacts who might be more willing to present the publicist's stories with greater prominence in exchange for exclusivity is equally important. So too is an awareness that this strategy or tactic can be a double-edged sword in that a media entity *not* receiving information on an exclusive basis may justifiably feel a need to be aggressive in covering a story from the *opposite* point of view—that is, seeking out sources who may not only not be sympathetic to the publicist's position, but who may also offer information strongly in contrast to it.

In such cases the publicist's best approach is to be fair, direct, helpful, and candid with the media that, while not being on the scene or in possession of information on an exclusive basis, still have a job to do. To the extent that the publicist can be of genuine assistance, this approach will likely work ultimately to the subject's advantage.

Frequently columnists, commentators, and others among the media will be so miffed at not being first or getting an exclusive—or, worse, seeing the exclusive go to a rival—that they might either ignore a subject or treat it in a dismissive manner, as if to suggest that if the particular media entity didn't have the story first, it wasn't worth reporting. Publicists must be aware, in such situations, to what degree such competitive considerations are significant among those media contacts that cover the publicist's subject areas or whose attention is sought. It is an important part of knowing your target market, when a part of that target is the media.

MEDIA UNDER THE INFLUENCE

Long-standing honorable tradition holds that there is an imaginary brick wall that separates the advertising sales department from the newsrooms of newspapers, magazines, and radio and television stations. That is to say, at no time will the media provide favorable or undeserved news coverage to their advertisers. Without a doubt, this rule is absolutely and unequivocally rigidly adhered to. Sometimes.

Major publications, such as *Time* and *Newsweek,* and newspapers of prominence, such as the *Wall Street Journal,* find the stakes are high, and the suggestion of advertisers' being given an advantage over nonadvertisers (or over competitors of the advertiser) could result in the kind of loss of professional standing and integrity from which the media might never recover. To the media, separating ads from news coverage is like separating church and state.

In certain situations, the lines between church and state are fading.

For example, some media observers have suggested that the ABC television network appears to provide a greater degree of attention to products, personalities, and events associated with its parent corporation, the Walt Disney Company. Similarly, Time Warner, which owns CNN and a host of other cable networks, as well as the powerhouse magazines *Time, Fortune, Sports Illustrated, People,* and *Entertainment Weekly,* may be suspected of working a bit more closely with media enterprises that are within the corporate family than those that are not.

Critics have charged that the films of Warner Brothers studios and products of related companies have an edge going in. Will *People, Time,* or CNN pan a Warner Brothers film, aware that to do so could result in the loss of millions of dollars in potential ticket sales and revenues to its corporate parent? Will Fox TV give a bad review to a Twentieth Century Fox release, or will *TV Guide* trash a Fox TV network show, or will any of them receive an unkind word from the editors of the *New York Post* or the *Village Voice,* as all of the entities are owned by the News Corporation (which, in turn, is owned by the reportedly very opinionated media baron Rupert Murdoch)?

Perhaps on occasion, but is it realistic to assume so on a frequent or consistent basis? Not as long as the corporate bottom lines have the influence that they do on daily operations—and that influence is considerable.

Fortune magazine has indeed published critical pieces on companies that have advertised in its pages (General Motors being a notable example, having promptly canceled its advertising contract with the magazine after the story ran, thus allowing *Fortune,* in turn, to highly publicize the occurrence, and receive huge amounts of favorable publicity in the process for maintaining its integrity at GM's expense).

Forbes has acted similarly, writing critically of various mutual fund companies that have advertised in its pages, for example.

As a general rule, however, count on the media to not be too harsh on their advertisers, claiming with a certain legitimacy, that, short of the advertiser's having committed the most dastardly of acts, such a policy is more of a reflection of fairness than favoritism. Maybe so.

In secondary media, most notably the trade press, the industry's church and state question is regarded in much the same way children's stories are remembered: with a certain warm fondness, but not to be taken literally. It is not at all uncommon for trade publications to not only provide a higher level of coverage to advertisers, but to, on some occasions, even make it a part of the advertising contract.

If, then, you are seeking to have your story appear in a trade publication where your competitor is a prominent advertiser, can you realistically expect equal treatment?

You can hope for it, but realistically, the competitor will have the edge—along with the ads. You can certainly make your case as to the newsworthiness of your message and ask to be treated fairly, but under the most common circumstances, those who can best afford the cost of having their message displayed most prominently will see their message displayed most prominently.

Under such circumstances, make certain that your material emphasizes your USPs—your unique selling points—making your story important, newsworthy, and virtually too good for the media to pass up. While it is right to be realistic about your chances of being overshadowed or upstaged by a well-financed competitor, emphasize in your media plan those entities that do tend to adhere (often in the face of tremendous pressure from advertisers) to a code of fairness and give good stories good play. There are enough of them to assure that if your message is a good one—and is well presented— your audience will be afforded the opportunity to receive it.

UNDERSTANDING MEDIA

Having found that the most efficient and effective method of getting a message to the most people in the shortest time is via the media, the publicist must either take a "shotgun" approach or pick and choose, but use the media to the strongest degree possible.

A publicist's objective is to get media attention for a particular subject: to make certain that the media know and understand the subject. But before that can take place, it is extremely important that the publicist understand the media. This is a more demanding task than many people assume it to be. Virtually every day, story ideas are being presented to editors or columnists, who respond in turn, "Have you ever *read* our paper?" Similarly, television producers are heard to ask publicists, "Have you ever *seen* our show?"

Woe to the publicist who must accept this dressing-down and admit not only to being unfamiliar with the particular entity but also to not having done his or her homework. If particular media people are worth your time to contact them to pitch your story, respect the fact that *their* time is equally valuable; don't waste it and insult them by not being familiar with their product and its standards and guidelines for accepting material.

While it may be every business leader's dream to see his or her name in the *Wall Street Journal,* the *New York Times, Fortune,* or *Forbes,* each of these publications has not only its own standards but also its own niche. Certain qualifications and attention to form must be addressed before the matter of meeting the standard even comes up.

Understand that "the media" is a plural term and gets more plural all the time. While "the newspaper" used to be a general, yet fairly specific, reference to one's own hometown daily paper, today's "newspaper" may be a national, regional, local, daily, weekly, mainstream, secondary, tabloid, or industry or trade-oriented publication. It may be free; it may be the only source of print news around; it may be fiercely competitive . . . or not.

Media exposure is the most obvious means by which a publicist can hope to generate the strongest, broadest exposure for a message. The assumption is that notice in the newspaper or being seen on TV will open the floodgates and reach the masses. While that theory is somewhat true in general, media, like the messages transmitted, come in a variety of shapes and sizes.

An Overview of the Most Accessible and Effective Media

Newspapers
  - national
  - daily and/or Sunday
  - trade daily, weekly, monthly, special edition
  - local (city, suburb, town, village, community)
  - specialty

Magazines
- news weeklies
- general interest
- consumer
- business
- city
- fraternal
- lifestyle, specialty magazines and journals
- ethnic
- sponsored specialty
- trade

Television
- network
- local
- cable
- satellite
- pay-per-view
- closed circuit
- in-flight
- in-store/point-of-sale
- video

Radio
- network
- local
- syndicated

Out-of-Home
- posters
- signs
- point-of-sale displays
- billboards
- airports, train stations, bus shelters

Newsletters
Internet/World Wide Web
Telephone
Mail (including E-mail and faxes)

The major daily national newspapers include:

Wall Street Journal
USA Today
Investor's Business Daily
Christian Science Monitor
Daily Variety
New York Times

Once the *Wall Street Journal* was considered a stuffy financial publication, consisting of business news, stock tables, and earnings reports. Today's *Wall Street Journal* is anything but stuffy, with crisp, intelligent, concise national and international news, features, and gossip. A show business celebrity is as likely to be profiled as a banker or corporate raider. While the paper strives for a business or financial connection to its subjects, the rules (if not the paper itself) have gotten more liberal. It is not at all uncommon to find film, television, and book reviews in the *Journal,* along with its coverage of the markets, royalty, the pope, and the Kennedy family. While the *Journal* is still aiming for a business audience, the quality of the paper's writing and general news coverage not only has increased its international prestige but also has made it a regular reading habit for a growing number of non-financially-oriented readers.

USA Today is Gannett's colorful national newspaper. Once described derisively as "McPaper" for its clearly aggressive attempt to appeal to the mass-market newspaper readers who were thought to prefer short summaries of news ("bites") rather than in-depth, thoughtful analysis, the paper has proven its worth and is now taken seriously by journalists and the public and is read and respected by a reasonably large audience. Its national focus and broad audience-appeal often make it the first choice for complimentary distribution at hotels and on major airlines.

Investor's Business Daily began in the 1970s as *Investor's Daily,* promoting itself as an alternative to the *Wall Street Journal.* It offered a heavy dose of exclusive financial data, often represented in charts and graphs, an emphasis on business news, and only the briefest summary coverage of news that its audience can get elsewhere. While the paper poses no threat to the *Journal's* prestige or dominance of its category, it is regarded as respectable and authoritative.

The *Christian Science Monitor* has long been looked to as having perhaps the most unbiased national and international news coverage of any newspaper in America. Its conservative appearance and its name have clearly limited both its appeal and its growth over the years, which is a shame because it is such a fine news product. Despite its perceived limitations, it remains highly respected and influential.

Daily Variety is, of course, the "show business bible," but it covers a good deal more than show business by covering so many businesses that border show business, such as real estate and finance, particularly as most entertainment companies are now owned and run by publicly held non-entertainment companies. General Electric owns NBC; Westinghouse owns CBS; Seagram's owns MCA/Universal; News Corporation owns Fox, and numerous music companies are owned by global financial partnerships. An important story in *Daily Variety* is likely to be picked up or reprinted by mainstream press around the world.

The *New York Times* national edition considers itself to be America's newspaper of record and regards the *Wall Street Journal* as its only real competition when it comes to business and financial news, and virtually no one else in any other category. Color has livened up the look of the newspaper industry's powerful "old gray lady," and the *Times* is arguably the most influential media entity in the United States.

There are other significant-circulation national newspapers with less influence than those just cited. The *International Herald Tribune* is the world's largest-circulation English-language newspaper, distributed in some 60 countries. Yet, its influence within the United States is only marginal, its global focus being far outside the range of subject interest of most mainstream American readers. The *Financial Times* is influential to a highly influential audience, and if that audience is your target group, the paper provides an excellent showcase. Perhaps 90 percent of the mainstream general audience, however, doesn't know it exists.

Most industries and professions with a significant number of participants have their own daily publications with names that are self-explanatory (such as *American Banker*). It is reasonable to conclude that, whatever the subject, business, or industry your message involves, there is likely a local or national (or both) daily publication that will be worthy of your consideration.

MORE ON MEDIA

While the media represent a hugely important part of getting publicity, it is not by any stretch the only part. Much of a publicist's working plan will often be described as a media plan, but it may include only a small amount of media appearances. It is worth mentioning as well that a media plan and a media schedule are not the same thing. Not everyone, even within the profession, understands this. Even at agencies, a request for a media plan will often be met with what appears to be an itinerary, or a list of publications or TV or radio programs either booked or pending. That's a schedule, a calendar.

A media plan outlines a schedule of targeted placements and defines how each item relates to the objective and to each other item, as well as the potential number of impressions made according to audience size, demographics, and related opportunities (both media and nonmedia).

For example, a publisher is sending an author into a major-market city to promote a new book. The complicated technical name for this is *city book tour.* The media schedule will show a list of contacts with times and dates, but the publicist's plan will show:

Objective: Generate maximum exposure and attention for the author and the book among demographically desirable target groups of potential buyers

- Arrange for signage with author and book photographs in bookstore(s) where the author will appear at a specific time to read from the book and sign copies; signage for such appearances typically remains in place for 10 to 14 days prior to the appearance and is positioned in store windows as well as in main traffic aisles and at checkout points/cash registers. Estimated exposure: dependent on the store location and seasonal traffic flow—potentially 2,000 to 4,000 people.

- Notices of the in-store appearance(s), with a press release and a photograph, are sent to local newspapers for listing in the "calendar of upcoming events" section one week prior to the appearance. Estimated exposure: each newspaper's circulation plus secondary readership.

- Appearances on local radio call-in shows to talk about (promote) the book, the author's work and career, and the upcoming local appearance. Estimated exposure: dependent on program audience, day part, and airtime. (This information available from each station's advertising sales office.)

- Copies of the author's book are made available in advance to local city magazine(s) and/or weekly newspaper(s), as well as to the larger-circulation daily newspaper(s) for a review to ideally coincide with the in-store appearance. Estimated exposure: combined circulation and secondary readership of publications that review the book or otherwise use the material provided.

• While in town, the author will visit a local school and talk with journalism students or staff of the school newspaper about careers in writing. Photos are distributed to local media, showing the author with the local students. (Note: depending on the subject of the book, the author might make a similar visit to a local hospital or health facility, union hall, veterans center, senior center, sports center, health club, shopping mall, or popular restaurant, with similar photo opportunities and media distribution.) Estimated exposure at the school: perhaps 20 to 50 people. Estimated exposure through secondary distribution of photos with captions: several thousand.

• A photo of the author and notice of the appearance is arranged for placement in future issues of the host organization's (school, health club, bookstore, etc.) newspaper, newsletter, or advertising. Estimated exposure: the approximate circulation of all published vehicles utilized.

• Following the bookstore appearance(s), the author signs additional copies of the book, to be displayed in the store(s) for a specified period of time following the appearance. Estimated exposure: dependent on location of store, positioning of display, seasonal volume of store traffic.

• Items (stories, anecdotes) of interest are provided to local columnists, relating experiences during the author's time spent in the area, naming local hotel, restaurants, and stopping points of interest to the columnists and audience [people want to both write about and read about subjects of interest to *them*—subjects to which they can relate and with which they are familiar], such as the author giving signed copies of the book to members of the hotel staff, a waiter, a cab driver, etc. Estimated exposure: newspaper circulation/readership of the columns.

• The author leaves behind signed books and any other personal items that might be used in fund-raising or auctions for charity in conjunction with a local columnist or radio station. Estimated exposure: the potential size of the target market/audience.

Note that pretty much every entry on the plan interrelates to the other entries, cross-referencing, supporting, extending, and maximizing the exposure. In-person appearances support the media opportunities, and media opportunities support the appearances.

Obviously the plan is easier to execute if the author is well known. But even without a well-known personality, by consistently, frequently, and prominently identifying him or her as simply "author of the new book on _____," interest will build in the book, the author's reputation will be greatly enhanced, and the author will *become* well known.

Publicists understand, perhaps better than anyone, that the way books, people, products, companies, issues, and causes become famous is by the public's being repeatedly and frequently exposed to them. We saw it on television, or on a sign in a store, or printed as a photo and caption in the newspaper. We've never met the person, we don't use the product, and yet we are aware, even familiar with it—all because someone created and worked a plan to publicize it.

NEWSPAPERS

Daily newspapers are typically the obvious top-of-mind targets of most publicists' efforts because these papers reach the largest general-interest audience on a daily basis, and unlike electronic media, they can be digested by the targeted audience at the individual audience member's convenience: over breakfast; on a bus, train, or plane; during lunch or coffee break; or at any other time the reader chooses to unwind, to look and learn. Newspaper reading is a habit, and despite the habit's having been pronounced dead on numerous occasions, newspapers remain very much alive and well.

There is also the matter of historic credibility. Entire generations grew up believing that something was both true and important if it was in the newspaper. Laying intellectual judgments on this point aside, publicists have in newspapers a media entity that must replenish its supply of fresh news on such a frequent basis that it is always receptive to ideas for stories. That's the theory, at least. In point of fact, major newspapers are anything but indiscriminate when it comes to what gets in and what's kept out. For this reason the publicist must, first, be clear and current on what types of information he or she can realistically expect a reporter or editor to accept, and second, work to establish and maintain a credible relationship with reporters and editors so that each story pitch can be judged on its merit without the constant reassessing of the publicist.

Most U.S. cities have at least one daily newspaper, and many have more than one, although the publicist may have to do a bit of homework to locate them and examine their individual profiles. Remember that just because a company's management—or, for that matter, its publicist—is not familiar with a particular paper, you can't assume it doesn't have a loyal readership or an impact.

For example, New York and Chicago newspaper readers often lament the loss of several of both cities' quality daily newspapers, victims of rising costs, heavy competition, and declining circulation. Yet, both cities still have numerous daily papers attempting to meet both general and very specialized tastes.

In Chicago, for example, the *Chicago Tribune* and the *Chicago Sun-Times* are the city's two largest-circulation, most-read daily papers. But even though the city's largest afternoon dailies folded years ago, the choices available to readers on a daily basis include the *Daily Herald* (circulation: 129,000), the *Daily Southtown* (circulation: 57,400), the *Chicago Defender* (circulation: about 20,000), and numerous foreign-language papers serving the area's bilingual and ethnic population. Most other large cities have similar "secondary" daily papers that, while not regarded as the city's "newspaper of record," nonetheless have loyal readers who may be the right group for a publicist's message.

Community, suburban, and weekly newspapers typically have neither the impact nor the circulation figures to match the big dailies. But to some publicists, concerned about their message's either being lost among the myriad stories in the bigger papers, reaching an audience with an already high "immunity" factor, or reaching an audience that is demographically outside of the target audience for the message, these more typically low-key publications do very well. There is also the added advantage of "shelf life." While it can't be said with certainty that each weekly edition is kept and referenced over a full week, surveys do suggest that the lack of immediacy of the weekly papers (versus the dailies) favors its remaining in circulation at least a few days longer.

Again using Chicago as an example, the *Chicago Reader* is one of some 200 weekly publications serving the area. With a circulation of 134,000, the *Reader* not only is known for insightful exposés and investigative reporting but also serves as a highly influential guide to area entertainment and nightlife. Concert, theater, and restaurant reviews are respected, and local businesses consider the publication as one to be taken seriously, despite its often counter-culture presentations and appearance. In New York, the *Village Voice* has had a similar influence and impact for decades, claiming a substantial national readership as well.

On a smaller scale, publicity targeted to a particular community newspaper may be of interest or value only to the members of that community, so its positioning relative to the publicist's message may be extremely well targeted.

While "specialty" newspapers can fill a niche and can appeal to a particular constituency (from the *Daily Worker*, founded more than a half century ago as the voice of the American socialist movement, to *Streetwise*, the newspaper created to raise funds for American homeless people), a major use for such low-circulation vehicles for today's publicist is in the form of *merchandising*. A story appearing in a small specialty paper can be recirculated either in reprint form or in its actual edition to generate a second round of exposure in direct mail, newsletters, or other newspapers that would not view the inclusion of such material as insulting or offensive from a competitive standpoint.

Another such "specialty" newspaper is one prepared for exclusive distribution at a conference, convention, or trade show. To the publicist seeking to gain attention for a particular product, issue, or other subject within the most influential industry circles, such a vehicle is ideal.

News Magazines

For all the talk that the magazine business was dying (talk that has persisted now for more than 30 years), the market seems as strong as ever. *Life, Look,* and the *Saturday Evening Post* may no longer dominate newsstands and coffee tables, but the major "news weeklies" *Time, Newsweek,* and *U.S. News & World Report* continue to not only reflect the climate of the times but also influence and "define" issues that often set the agenda for mainstream America.

It was once regarded as the ultimate coup if a publicist was credited with securing coveted cover stories in *Time* and *Newsweek* in the same week, as was the case for singer Bruce Springsteen in October of 1975. Never before to anyone's recall had a pop performer achieved such status without having to die for it.

On a smaller level, closer to home, each week the "big three" news weeklies sort through press releases on the widest possible range of subjects and listen to pitches from publicists representing corporate America (and elsewhere), and industries from health care to travel to agriculture, entertainment, finance, and politics. Contrary to popular opinion, the major weekly news magazine editors and writers do have telephones, fax machines, and E-mail. They do get calls from publicists on a regular basis, and they do use material provided to them by contacts (publicists) outside of the publications' own paid staffs.

They are reachable.

Is it realistic to think that a local political candidate or community event, or a product or service largely of interest to a narrow geographical or demographic audience would be of interest to a national news weekly?

Probably not—*unless* there is something of unique, special, or human interest tied to it.

• In the South, a woman who worked her whole life as a cleaning lady saved more than $170,000, which she gave away to create a scholarship fund for poor children to go to college. It wasn't national politics, film, or high-level corporate mischief, but all news weeklies printed the story.

• A local hospital opened a modest satellite facility in Oak Park, Illinois, calling it a Women's Health and Wellness Center, specializing in health issues of women from sports injuries to stress-related illness to pregnancy. A press release and fact sheet were distributed . . . and *Time* magazine printed the story.

What a local school may be doing to improve the environment, a company offering employees innovative on-site child care, students giving up free time to work on a crisis help line, a senior citizen realizing a lifelong dream to perform with the local symphony orchestra . . . These are examples of small local stories that could be included in national news weeklies, if the stories are brought to the magazines' attention.

How do the subjects and the people who are profiled in cover stories and articles in the national news magazines happen to get that coverage? It doesn't just happen. The staff members of the publication don't just *run across* such subjects. More often than not, a persuasive publicist has been persistently pressing for the story to be covered.

Is it realistic to think that a small community banker, merchant, manufacturer, or practitioner in some remote area could end up on the cover of *Forbes* or *Fortune* magazine?

Realistic may not be the right word, but if the person or business can be shown to have created, implemented, bought, or sold a product of interest, or to have paid a price for *not* having done any of these things, bringing such information to the editor's attention can pay off and may very well result in the highly prized cover.

It is true that the chairmen of GM, IBM, ITT, AT&T, MCA, and AOL will still get their phone calls returned first, but consider the number of times an unknown computer whiz kid, a small-town inventor, or the creator of a new and promising multilevel marketing program for vitamins turns up on the cover of a national news weekly, Sunday supplement, or city magazine, and you hear someone ask, "How did they ever find *that* guy?"

The answer is almost always a case of *that guy* finding *them*—or at least a case of that guy's publicist finding them.

The Magazine Marketplace

The magazine industry is broad, and each year, as magazines fail, new ones are launched quickly to fill the void, such as it may be. This presents a huge landscape of opportunities for publicists. As with newspapers geared to serve the special interests of particular industries and professions, no matter what the subject, there is likely to be one or more magazines to address it.

For example, as controversial and socially unacceptable as cigarette smoking had become by the 1990s, cigar smoking not only enjoyed a return to fashion but also inspired several magazines which could quickly boast very respectable circulation figures. *Cigar* magazine, *Cigar Aficionado,* and *Smoke* were among the most successful.

How long can anyone read a magazine about cigars, and how much is there to say? More important to the subject at hand, how can this benefit publicists? The answer to all three questions is: More than one might think.

Publicists representing restaurants, hotels, trade associations, entertainers—even movie actresses—were finding ways to relate to the subject and were lining up to place material in the magazines, where all that it appeared was necessary was the presence of a cigar.

For publicists the requirement should be to deliver not a story about cigars, but rather *a story of interest to cigar smokers* that these specialty publications would find too good to reject.

Philip Morris Magazine, a sponsored specialty magazine, similarly aims its product at a mailing list of thousands of people who are, presumably, smokers. In between news and feature stories built around smokers and the issue of smokers' rights are articles on a wide range of interests, intended to remind readers (and regulators and legislators) that smokers are people of very diverse interests, not just "smokers." For the publicist, such narrow specialty publications still offer an opportunity, if the audience that the magazine reaches is the audience the publicist wants. The publicist doesn't have to be representing a tobacco-related product or even have a position one way or another about smoking. The objective is to reach an audience with a message, and if a particular "specialty" publication delivers that audience, whatever else it does (within reason) does not have to concern the publicist.

As specialty magazines go, there is no shortage of publications dealing with the celebration of marriage. Such titles as *Bride, Modern Bride, Elegant Bride, Bridal Guide,* and *Wedding Bells* are only a few entries on the very long list of publications to which a publicist can direct a varied assortment of messages on health, finance, food, entertaining, clothing, gardening, and much more. Again, it is not a matter of having a message *about* brides, as much as a message of something of value *to* brides.

While few brides would want to know about it, statistics and reality led to the success of *Divorce* magazine, with a circulation of some 83,000 by the end of its second year. Remaining true to its name but taking a generally positive approach to lifestyle issues, the magazine has offered articles with such titles as "Meditation: How It Works," "Stress Busters," "Safe at Home," and "Jump Start: Back to School." As with a bride magazine, a magazine aimed at an audience of divorcées shows publicists that articles on almost any subject are appropriate articles for these readers, who are people with a multitude of interests.

Fraternal magazines tend to be overlooked by publicists, and that's a mistake. Most fraternal organizations have their own publications, subsidized by a portion of the members' annual dues or membership fee. Members reportedly look forward to receiving and reading the publications on a regular basis, often in a very relaxed (susceptible) frame of mind. This is an excellent time for publicists to present a message. Assuming the fraternal organization's membership fits within the publicist's demographic target group's parameters, this represents a potentially large and receptive audience.

Some specialty trade publications, such as the *Journal of the American Medical Association,* have become so influential as to be frequently referenced in national general-interest reports in major newspapers and on network television and radio news programs. A bylined article in *JAMA* is widely recognized as important as well as prestigious, with reprints keeping most of its articles alive virtually indefinitely, to be circulated and quoted again and again. *JAMA* is a uniquely influential vehicle, serving also as a model of what most trade associations wish their magazines or newsletters could be. While presenting significant articles and reviews, the publication also reinforces and promotes the image of the American Medical Association as the preeminent professional group in its field.

Publicists studying such a model can see the power of a trade journal when it is so well done. It promotes the trade group to "the rest of the world," influences leaders within the profession itself, and raises awareness and credibility of people and products presented within its pages.

In the best of all situations, the message, target audience, and publication are a perfect match. Sometimes the delivery system is more subtle. For example, a simple passing reference by a doctor contributing a major article to a medical journal might take note of an innovative computer software program used in his or her research. The publicist representing the software company should exploit the reference. The same article might make a small reference to an investor or benefactor who helped to fund the research, and the publicist for the benefactor might want to use that reference to gain goodwill.

To some companies and clients, being the focal point of a media story is neither necessary nor even particularly desirable. Instead, merely being *included* in a story as the creator, manufacturer, distributor, or marketer of a particular piece of equipment that made something important happen is acknowledgment enough. Such public recognition may then be incorporated as an endorsement, of sorts, in sales presentations or literature.

Modern Maturity magazine has a more commercial look and feel than a prestigious journal but is, in its way, no less powerful or influential. As the official publication of the American Association of Retired Persons (AARP), *Modern Maturity* boasts an enormous circulation, targeting the "mature market" (persons who used to be called senior citizens or older people).

Actually the organization's name (if not the publication's) is a bit of a misnomer, as AARP begins inviting people to sign on at age 50. While at that age they may be showing signs of maturity, few are retired, and nothing requires that either members or readers be American.

No matter; the publicist seeking to reach a mature audience (an older demographic) for a message oriented to health, travel, leisure activities, entertainment, investments, or social or political issues and causes would find this publication's readership, with its reported circulation in the tens of millions, an excellent and credible showcase.

Modern Maturity tells a lot, with its title alone, about what the magazine offers and who makes up its audience. The same could be said for such publications as *Working Woman* and *Working Mother*. Editors of these magazines would like it if publicists brought them stories that stay true to the name and theme of the magazine, but of greater importance is that the subject be one that will have appeal to the publication's primary audience.

While city magazines vary widely in circulation, prestige, influence, and quality, for certain subjects in certain markets, they can be enormously useful. These are the publications that can always count on an audience for issues on the "10 Best Restaurants," the "Best Places to Go for a Year-Round Tan," the "Best Dressed," and "Worst Dressed," lists—and such subject matter, and almost anything related to it, qualifies as wide-open opportunities for publicists. An aggressive publicist, incidentally, will push not only for his or her subject's inclusion on an established list, but also for the creation of a list that's virtually constructed around his or her subject.

New York magazine has helped to advance numerous people, places, and causes over the years with an emphasis on food, fashion, the arts, and politics. *Chicago* magazine has a significant upscale audience that attaches considerable credibility to the magazine's recommendations. To be profiled in its pages labels the subject as important to a constituency that is itself regarded as important. Such positioning is of particular value to a budding entrepreneur, entertainer, politician, or mogul who seeks the attention of a select group of "insiders" whose awareness of a presence can help accelerate the rate of its acceptance and greater exposure.

Los Angeles, San Francisco, Philadelphia, Houston, Detroit, and Minneapolis are some of the cities that can claim established, relatively influential city magazines that are good enough to be read by people in other cities. A publicist can generate exposure going city by city, using these publications to build a "grassroots" base on which to build a greater level of awareness.

Depending on the objective and strategy, a single publication or a mix could be considered. That is, in certain situations, a single story, profile, or article in *Redbook, Business Week, Consumer Reports, Kiplinger's Personal Finance,* or *People,* included in media kits and mailings, will serve in and of itself to attract the attention of other media, as well as of a specific target audience.

In other instances, a mix of placements in a more numerous and diverse group of publications might be a more effective strategy to create the desired level of awareness and image of credibility.

Whether the publicist's approach is to exclusively use a single, well-chosen, targeted publication to reach its audience, or working a combination of media placements, over a longer period of time or a highly concentrated period, the range of magazine choices and opportunities is vast.

SOUND AND PICTURES

The publicist who woke up smiling was probably having that dream again: the one that has the bookers from *The Today Show, Oprah Winfrey,* and *Larry King Live* all calling within an hour of each other to say, "OK, we've got your story booked for tomorrow. Wear your blue shirt." Such is the power of television—virtually *any* television, from local to network to cable.

MSNBC, the cable television joint venture of NBC Television and Microsoft, used as a slogan in its news hour promotions ". . . not your father's news show." Shortly afterward, Great Britain's BBC, in launching its newest channel, announced, "This is not your grandfather's BBC."

These entities would, of course, like their target audiences of young adults to believe that they represent a departure from traditional, mainstream local and network television programming. In point of fact, network TV standards of old still largely guide the standards and practices of modern cable, satellite, and Internet systems—especially after they have amassed a sizable audience and come to understand how much they have to lose by pushing the standards too far.

Ironically, MSNBC is very much like your father's TV viewing choices, its programming virtually identical to the attractive-news-reader-behind-a-desk format and "roundtable" talk shows in the style of those pioneered by David Susskind and Irv Kupcinet in the 1950s and 1960s.

What *has* changed is the longer list of choices and the fact that few of them even attempt to appeal to the mass audiences that ABC, CBS, and NBC had targeted from television's infancy through its "golden age" and on into the 1970s. The proliferation of niches and special-interest channels and networks has created opportunities for television exposure of publicists' messages as were previously available only through the most focused and limited-circulation magazines.

While a publicist's fantasy is to arrange showcase appearances on high-visibility, powerful network shows, such as *The Today Show* and *Good Morning America,* and syndicated national programs on the order of *Oprah Winfrey* and *Live with Regis and Kathie Lee,* cable television opportunities abound with the channels themselves, before even getting into the actual programming. The cable systems, growing each year, include:

A&E (Arts & Entertainment) Network
Animal Network
BET (Black Entertainment Television)
Bloomberg News Service
Bravo!
CMT (Country Music Television)
CNBC
CNN (Cable News Network)
CNNfn (CNN financial news)
CNN Headline News
CNN/SI (CNN and *Sports Illustrated*)
Comedy Central
C-Span
C-Span 2
Discovery Channel
E! Entertainment Television
ESPN (Entertainment and Sports Network)
ESPN 2
ESPNews
Fox Family Channel
The Food Channel
Fox News Channel
Fox Sports Net
Gameshow Channel
The Golf Channel

Health Network
The History Channel
Home Shopping Network
Knowledge TV
The Learning Channel
local public access channels
Lifetime ("Television for Women")
MEU (Mind Extension University)
MSNBC (Microsoft/NBC)
MTV (Music Television)
The Nostalgia Channel
The Outdoor Channel
Ovation
QVC Network
Speed (motor/auto channel)
TBS (Atlanta-based "superstation")
TNN (The Nashville Network)
Travel Channel
USA Network
VH1 (Music Television)
The Weather Channel
WGN (Chicago-based "superstation")

In some cases opportunities lie deeper within a cable network in unlikely places. The "news channels" with a wide schedule of talk shows and magazine shows are fairly obvious choices for most publicists' hit lists, but a bit of research will reveal that the music-video channels MTV and VH1 also have news, magazine, and fashion programs, focusing on the arts and often politics: two subject categories with a very wide range. Note to publicists: Find your hook, and make it fit the format.

Cable's Bravo! network is largely considered a showcase for foreign films, art films, ballet, and opera. In addition to that programming, however, the channel offers interviews and film-school "seminars" in which actors, writers, and directors review their own work and the work of others.

An enterprising publicist who is not able to get his or her message placed as the central theme of a program might well be able to place a message within the program nonetheless: a director may freely make references to anything from the kind of cars used in the film, to the bank that helped arrange financing, to Federal Express rushing prints to previews and saving the day.

Placing the message in less obvious spots than between two other commercials is more likely to result in both notice and recall. Publicists: Find your hook and make it fit the format.

The Nashville Network, BET, and Comedy Central all offer a specific variety of talk shows and interview shows, providing a forum for guests and subjects that can be made to seem relevant to the particular audience by sheer virtue of their inclusion in the programs.

It is not that complicated for publicists to review the issue from both sides. That is, first, consider which programs, stations, networks, and cable channels present the best possible showcase placements for the intended message, and second, consider how the message can be fine-tuned or adapted, if necessary, to be more appealing or interesting for the audiences of the media that might *not* have been on the list of targeted media. Find your hook and make it fit the format.

Jude Wanniski, in his *Media Guide: A Critical Review of the Media,* notes that "While pictures complement a newspaper article, television can't seem to tell a story without them, relying on visuals to *make* the story, even when there is nothing new to report."

C-SPAN: TV IN THE PUBLIC INTEREST

C-Span and C-Span 2 were once regarded as perhaps the dullest of public-service channels, fixing a stationary camera on a meeting of the Congress, state legislature, or city council and allowing politicians to go on endlessly, causing viewers who paused at the channel for even a short while to long for commercial interruptions. By the mid-1990s, C-Span had built a loyal and growing audience, appealing in part to TV watchers who are avid fans of talk radio.

While C-Span is firmly committed to devoting large blocks of time to legislative sessions, programs such as the morning news briefing *Washington Journal* provide a forum for reporters from the U.S. and foreign press to discuss the most specific subjects (health care, aviation, communications, banking, education, child care, etc.) as well as the most general of matters (current affairs, world history). The journalists are often joined (or replaced) by lobbyists and legislators both in the studio and via telephone, reflecting and representing the views of every conceivable interest group.

A typical hour of *Washington Journal* may find agents of tobacco interests debating cigarettes and health with health-care professionals, auto-industry spokespersons sharing the desk with safety experts, women's rights advocates taking on religious fundamentalists, manufacturers versus consumer advocates, and on and on. Viewers from around the United States call in to participate in the discussion.

Beyond the legislative sessions, C-Span also takes its camera into meetings of Citizens for Cleaner Air, the Center for Integrity in Government, Advocates for Better Schools, Parents for Better Television, and the like, sometimes even attending meetings where the speakers address the audience in Chinese, Spanish, Japanese, or French, with a translation provided.

In the interests of fairness, the seemingly broadest possible range of associations, parties, organizations, and coalitions is likely to have one or more of its meetings covered by C-Span (taped and repeated several times over a week) and can invite participation from any number of people who may have a message relevant to a specific subject deemed to be in the public interest. For the publicist, it may not be *The Today Show,* but it is a loyal, intelligent audience and an opportunity. Find your hook and make it fit the format.

Far from being exclusively the domain of politicians that it once was, C-Span will routinely visit such spots as a printing plant in Tennessee or the Abraham Lincoln Bookstore in Chicago. The network might also carry a speech by an executive, an industry leader, a representative or spokesperson, or a private citizen whose appearance and coverage of his or her subject is based on a supposition that audiences will be the better for it.

C-Span subjects have included stamp collecting, cartooning, architecture, personal computer applications, and gun control. A publicist who cannot find a way to present his or her subject for a C-Span segment isn't really trying.

In an effort to get outside of its broadcast studio and offer alternatives to legislators' talking heads, C-Span will frequently put its camera in the broadcast booth of a popular talk-radio program and show the audience what such programs actually look like. In these instances the subject of the program reaches an even larger audience, in effect being simulcast on TV and radio. In terms of ratings, the numbers may be small, but the impact of these programs has registered with the public.

Booknotes—an extremely popular, regular Sunday-night program in which a guest speaks without commercial interruption for an hour on the subject of his or her book and related matters—is to C-Span what *Masterpiece Theater* is to PBS.

To many people, C-Span is an acquired taste and is regarded as the distributor of the type of intellectual programming that public television stations offered before they had tapes of *Barney, Monty Python's Flying Circus,* and *Riverdance.* Some may regard it as pretty dull stuff—and certainly it seems that, judging by some of the callers, its audience has the occasional flying-saucer passenger—but legions of regular viewers (who pay for cable service) find it very rich. To the publicist it is one more wide-open opportunity.

PUBLIC ACCESS TV: FOR ANYONE, BUT NOT FOR EVERYONE

Without question, for some television viewers, the ultimate exercise in self-indulgence is the cable television public access channel. This is a different channel with different programs customized for each individual city's or community's cable system, although the cable companies sometimes swap tapes with one another.

Local cable regulators require that cable systems carry public access channels the way the FCC used to require public service programming. A major difference between the two examples is that the public service programs were (and often still are) usually pretaped interviews with a local pastor or the deputy water commissioner, and the tapes were shown at about 4 A.M.

Public access channels, on the other hand, are full-time channels, sometimes 24 hours, turned over to local folks (they don't even have to be cable television customers) within the cable system's viewing area. "Turned over" means typically that by simply signing up to reserve a time slot, a local member of the community may use the time allotted for pretty much any purpose he or she chooses. Routinely the "programs" include, ah, pretaped interviews with the local pastor and the deputy water commissioner . . . but they also include local gallery owners, poets, artists, and art dealers; the local school's glee club, choir, or dance class; local awards and recognition ceremonies; school sports; people from the community offering their own theater or movie reviews or just interviewing one another; and at least a few ambitious folks hoping to be spotted and, perhaps, become the next Joan Rivers or David Letterman.

Although the "programs"—and, to some people, even the concept itself—may seem pretty lame, public access television does have an audience. Like C-Span, some public access channels put a camera on radio programs in progress. Bruce DuMont, host of the political radio talk show *Beyond the Beltway,* says he is often approached by people who recognize him from their local cable system's presentation of his radio show.

Such, at whatever level, is the power of television, and such is the opportunity public access TV channels afford publicists.

Normally cable systems have guidelines that must be followed, such as that the program's content must be something worthwhile, although obviously that is a relative term. It cannot be a commercial (or even an infomercial) for anything. Occasionally the subjects that do make it to the home screen are surprisingly controversial and push the limits of free speech, such as when the Ku Klux Klan appeared to have a fairly regular half hour each week on public access cable in several markets. The fact that these segments were not only presented but also talked about on talk radio and in other media proves the potential influence that appearing on public access channels can have.

Some commercial enterprises, such as the largest and best-known companies and businesses, should not be represented on public access television, even if their subjects meet all of the local cable system's requirements. The reason for this is that mature brands and issues of a certain type need to be presented in a carefully managed environment, mindful of what appears before and after them. It would not do, for example, for a spokesperson for Procter & Gamble to be interviewed after a half hour of "At Home with the Imperial Wizard of the KKK."

Is there anyone who *would* want that spot?

Probably not. But some companies would have a higher price to pay than others, if for no other reason than the common knowledge that they had the financial resources to afford to be somewhere other than public access television.

But a community group with a cause, an event to be promoted, a demonstration of a product of educational value to young people, a point of view on a subject of public interest—all might benefit from exposure on public access TV. Perhaps not *only* on public access TV, but as a part of the media mix.

Local TV

Legendary political figure Thomas P. "Tip" O'Neill is reported to have said that "all politics is local," meaning that no matter how important an issue or story may seem to be, it is only as important as the degree to which each individual at a local level *perceives* that importance. It is another way of saying, "So, how does this affect *me*?"

Local television, by its very definition, focuses as much as possible on local people, places, and things, covering events outside of the local market only to the extent that they captivate audiences to a huge degree, and even then, trying to relate to them only in a local way:

• A public building in Oklahoma City is devastated by a terrorist bomb, and the television audience is riveted to the story. Were any of the people who were killed or injured local people from the town that is home base to the local TV station? Were any of the victims relatives of local citizens who can be interviewed to put a local connection to the story?

• An airplane crash kills 200 people. Were any of the victims local? Were any of them relatives of local people? Had the plane stopped in the local market for refueling? Had any of the crew members ever lived in the local market or attended school there?

An earthquake in San Francisco, a subway disaster in New York, a fire in Brazil, a political scandal, the Olympics, a film that opens to great reviews—a local TV station's first responsibility is to explore whether or not there is a possible local connection.

In the category of local television, most every midsize or larger city—and a fair number of small ones—has at least one local TV station, even if it is a cable or UHF station. It used to be that the programming on these stations largely comprised reruns of old movies and off-network series, as they represented the absolute cheapest programming material available. By the late 1990s these same stations were running news and public affairs shows instead of, or in addition to, such programming, finding that they were more appealing to local audiences and helped to build a loyal viewership for the station. A host or moderator, a plant, and a couple of armchairs or a desk form the basis of potentially profitable programming, as well as opportunities for publicists.

Citizens lobbies or special-interest groups may complain that local news programs typically present pretty much only local *bad* news to a disproportionate degree. The *New York Times Magazine,* in a cover story titled "Does Local TV News Have to Be So Bad?," noted, "Local TV news is more and more about crime and violence. One station in Orlando tried to take the high road. Its biggest obstacle? The viewers."

It will surprise few people to learn that bad news pulls higher ratings than good news and, despite claims to the contrary, violence on TV attracts a larger audience than coverage of the local flower show.

"Good TV reporting takes tremendous drive and energy, strong visuals and you have to look good," comments *Times* writer Michael Winerip.

Publicists seeking to place a story on a local news show must know two things: first, that they are competing with every other publicist and, more important, with every other bit of news and information that may be under consideration for the newscast, and second, that the producer, editor, or programmer may *prefer* to give the publicist's story the edge but finds the color and drama of some other stories to be more compelling. In such situations the publicist cannot take an attitude that just being there is a strong enough hook. Echoing the words of Winerip, the publicist must present "tremendous drive and energy, strong visuals . . . and look good."

Equality cannot be the rule in television or any other medium. Just being as good as the other stories under consideration doesn't make the cut. If all stories appear to be equally interesting or worthwhile, the one with the greatest number of "strongly visual" elements will move ahead. If all stories are equally visual, the one with the most prominent or well-known people or other subject pegs (landmark building, highly trafficked location, distinguished history, children, great-looking people) has the edge. It goes back to the USP—the unique selling point—to make the equally good story the breakout story. And to the publicist: Find your hook and make it fit the format.

CLOSED-CIRCUIT TV: WHO'S WATCHING?

Channel One—TV in the classroom—was an ambitious, expensive, and controversial closed-circuit television project that rolled along on shaky ground for years. Perhaps one day, like the cellular phone, such a programming system will find acceptance at a manageable cost. The Financial Satellite Network (FSN) was a similarly innovative setup that offered closed-circuit programming to brokerage firms and financial institutions that subscribed to the service. Based in Dallas, much of the programming was good and useful, but television in the workplace, even for training sessions, remains a dubious element with a very uneven record of success.

While a number of businesses, schools, and religious organizations use some form of closed-circuit TV to limited degrees, perhaps the only truly successful applications have been in hotels and resorts (a channel of local attractions, entertainment options, and services menus) and CNN's Airport Channel, where passengers awaiting their flights sit, stand, or pace—a near-captive audience—as television screens that offer only one choice of channels present selected news, sports, features, and commercials.

One of the most innovative closed-circuit TV systems is the TeleSuite Network, a unique form of videoconferencing available at participating Hilton hotels. One party to an interview or meeting sits at literally *half* of a table, in front of a decorative backdrop, looking at a mirror. As the connection is made, another party to the interview or meeting takes the place of the mirror, seated at what appears to be the other half of the table and in front of an identical backdrop. The two sides appear to look at each other and talk to each other as if they were actually sitting across the table from one another. Sound and picture quality are excellent. For the actor or author out to publicize a new project, an old-fashioned cross-country media tour and series of one-on-one, face-to-face interviews can be accomplished in hours, rather than weeks, with the actor or author never having to leave a chair. And as the old expression goes, what's good for the actor is just as effective with a CEO talking with financial reporters, politicians talking with their constituent media, entrepreneurs, or virtually anyone else who would seek publicity via the interview or media tour.

Adaptations of this format—and merchandising its results— are virtually limited only by a publicist's imagination. Clearly, it is not prime time on NBC, but it is a potentially viable and creative media tool. The next best thing to being there? In some respects, maybe better.

NEWSLETTERS

If television and newspapers are sought for their tremendous reach, power, and impact, and magazines are sought for their prestige, longer shelf life, and perceived influence, newsletters may well be the quiet giant of media.

Some newsletters are available for the asking, others for the price of a subscription. Still other newsletters may be acquired only by subscribing to or purchasing a particular product or service, to which the newsletter is represented as an incentive or "value-added" item.

Publicists should consider newsletters on two levels of action:

- Pursue article or story placements as one might use any other targeted media.
- Develop and distribute a newsletter of the company's or subject's own, as an alternative communications form, similar to an advertorial or infomercial.

Newsletters, while often published and circulated by huge, global media conglomerates, are also published by individuals with names like Bob and Peggy, literally working from personal computers on their kitchen tables. If the content is written well, few readers can tell the difference between the finished products of Bob or Peggy and those of McGraw-Hill.

To publicize a message using *Securities Week* or the *Wall Street Letter* is to reach a key group of participants in the securities, brokerage, and financial services industry. Subscribers to these newsletters have a greater-than-passing interest in the subject and are willing to pay premium rates to receive information that they perceive not everyone else is getting. From the publicists' point of view, these vehicles thus become highly desirable placements for the suggestion of added importance attached to their contents. Reaching the editors and writers for these publications is exactly the same process as reaching their counterparts at the mass-circulation publications. The publicists' challenge is to make the subject seem important enough to be covered by a publication that owes its audience something it can't get on any newsstand.

While many readers of the newsletters may also read the major high-circulation publications such as *Business Week, Fortune,* or the *Wall Street Journal,* a suggestion of the audience's perceived value of the newsletters is reflected in their cost. An annual subscription to *Securities Week* may be more than 10 times that of *Business Week.*

The most quoted source on the evening news throughout the "oil crisis" of the 1970s was *Platt's Oilgram*—an industry newsletter.

When the stock market was dropping with the velocity of a broker jumping out of a window, the first publication to claim to be the publication of record, having forecast the crash, was a virtually "shoestring" newsletter published by financial advisor Joe Granville.

And when publicists want to know what's going on in the field of public relations, the first stop is usually *Jack O'Dwyer's Newsletter,* the New York–based newsletter that has been taking and reporting the pulse of the industry for decades.

Yet, when competing with choice targets such as *USA Today, Business Week, People,* or a segment on *CBS Sunday Morning,* newsletters rank as among the most overlooked areas of the media mix—often so seemingly irrelevant and insignificant as to *not justify a place in the media plan.*

This is a huge mistake.

Not only do established newsletters reach key individuals in nearly every profession and industry, but also newsletters created and produced by publicists representing their clients are regarded as an extremely effective and respectable do-it-yourself publishing venture.

• Conservative commentator and radio talk-show host Rush Limbaugh publishes the *Limbaugh Letter* to promote his conservative views and, not incidentally, his radio program, speaking engagements, videos-for-sale, and so forth.

• Steven J. Nash Publishing Company offers the *James Kavanaugh Newsletter* to a combination of paid and unpaid subscribers as a vehicle to promote the author-poet-theologian's books, tapes, views, and appearances.

• The *Newsletter of the National Alliance of Futures and Options Brokers, Traders and FCMs* provides a monthly forum for its members to present news and opinions of great importance within the futures and financial services industry.

• Thomas L. Harris, Northwestern University professor, head of the consulting firm of Thomas L. Harris & Company, and a founder of Golin/Harris Communications, also publishes the quarterly *MPR update,* a much-anticipated and highly regarded newsletter that addresses successes, failures, and interesting developments in the area of marketing public relations.

As innumerable entrepreneurs, corporations, trade associations, and fan clubs have learned:

- There is a huge real and potential market for newsletters and a wide-open array of prime opportunities for publicists to reach and influence their audiences.
- The cost of producing a newsletter is modest by almost any standard.
- Newsletters are perhaps the most respectable form of self-publishing.

- In many respects newsletters offer the same benefits as advertising: the ability to control the message content, space, creative presentation, and timing, while, if done well, appearing far more dignified and authoritative than an ad or a commercial.

So, if newsletters are so versatile and effective, why aren't they given more respectful and prominent treatment in the media plan?

A reasonable answer is that it's because so many publicists, like ad executives, regard newsletters not as media, but as collaterals— on an equal level with brochures and mailing pieces. A good case can be made that they're either or both.

Radio

Like newspapers and magazines, radio is a medium that has been pronounced dead more than once, only to bounce back stronger than ever. AM-radio was the place where disc jockeys played records, listeners called in requesting songs, hits were made, and musical tastes were shaped.

In the modern era, stations on the FM-band play music for every taste. AM and FM are both home to the "talk radio" phenomenon, and NPR—National Public Radio—long regarded as one long public-service announcement, is a political, social, and cultural powerhouse from coast to coast.

For the publicist, radio is a field of opportunities as wide as the band of stations itself. And, while some members of the audience are still in their bathrobes while listening to the radio, a large number of radio personalities likewise are wearing their bathrobes while they are on the air, often broadcasting from their homes, hotels, or assorted locations. Through modern technology, no one even suspects that the program host is not ensconced in a studio. Computer advances allow an interviewer to lead a panel discussion from Washington, D.C., that includes panelists in New York, Chicago, and

London, with each voice having the clarity of that of an in-studio participant.

Talk radio offers a forum for guests to present their subjects, and call-in segments permit a guest's supporters to join, lead, or influence a discussion. Critics may call in with challenges, but unlike television, there are no startled or nervous facial expressions, and troublemakers can be eliminated at the push of a button.

If a publicist is not successful at booking a subject on a program, the publicist or another designated spokesperson can still call in to radio shows and plug a product, promote a cause or issue, counter a competitor, or otherwise influence a discussion.

If NPR carries your story, the story takes on the stamp of major importance to a large segment of the national audience. And the range of subjects is unlimited. The audience for *Morning Edition* gets a mix of general news, political analysis, film, theater, science, technology, finance, ethnic news from bureaus around the world, and snippets of music with long pieces on what was or is behind the music, from folk and jazz to classical, rock, and New Age. *All Things Considered* is the evening drive-time counterpart and mirror to *Morning Edition.*

In between these two highly rated shows are interviews, commentaries, and panel discussions, taking on the Middle East, pet care, child care, law, feminism, and food. A publicist with essentially any subject should be able to find a place in the NPR day part. Do your homework, find your niche, find your hook, approach the segment producer, and pitch your ideas.

AT A GLANCE
DIFFERENT STROKES: UNDERSTANDING MEDIA

- Media are not always objective regarding a subject. Know their prejudices, leanings, and predisposition, and compensate accordingly.

- Most media still compete aggressively for *scoops* and *exclusives*. Exclusives can frequently be negotiated for favorable positioning.

- A good reporter will ask questions of a competitor or rival after getting information or an interview from you. Anticipate this, and plan appropriate comments to address criticism.

- More effective publicity results from a publicist having cultivated relationships with members of the intensely competitive media.

- With some exceptions, advertisers actually do get favorable treatment from the media—or, at the very least, a greater degree of *fairness* than nonadvertisers.

- Don't insult members of the media by approaching them to publicize your subject while you are still largely unfamiliar with the format, focus, or standards of their individual properties.

- Most industries and professions have their own daily and/or weekly trade publications. Do not aim so high for major media that you neglect the influential trade media close to home.

continued

- Your media plan outlines a schedule of targeted media contacts and placements, and defines how each contact enhances and supports the overall program.

- People believe what they read—that if they see it in writing, it must be true. Whether it is a press release, a fact sheet, a media alert, a survey, a study, or the end result of your efforts—a story or article printed in a newspaper or a magazine—seeing the words in writing represents a credibility that other formats have still not achieved.

- Specialty magazines—whether their focus is cigars, Beanie Babies, or an Elvis commemorative—are well read and tend to have a longer "shelf life" because of the very suggestion that there is something special about them. They also afford the opportunity to widely circulate an article without its being viewed as a competitive story with most other media. This makes them a particularly desirable, yet often overlooked, vehicle for publicists.

- Take note of which programs, stations, networks, or cable systems provide the best showcase for your subject, in terms of coverage and response. Put greater emphasis on this venue in follow-up stories.

- Infomercials are a double-edged sword. They are paid ads disguised to look like television shows and newscasts. To be the subject of an infomercial, or even to be referenced in one, affords visibility, but too often at the expense of *credibility*.

continued

- Bad news gets more attention and better ratings than good news. Be mindful that, in asking the media to make your subject the focus of a story, the media typically seek a comment, a reaction, or even an opposing opinion from known critics, competitors, opponents, or rivals, in an effort to "spice up" a story with controversy.

- Newsletters are the "quiet giant" of media, having high readership scores, credibility, and a high pass-along rate. A newsletter is also another example of a media vehicle that is regarded as largely nonthreatening and noncompetitive to other media (with the possible exception of another newsletter). Whether your subject is included in the newsletter of someone else or you publish your own, this is a highly effective vehicle.

4

Creating Opportunities

In television, radio, and print news, the ability of a news organization to have a reporter "on the scene" has become increasingly more important, as well as being a highly competitive consideration.

While it has become a bit of a joke over the years, it is still regarded as essential nonetheless that a TV reporter reporting national news be shown standing on the lawn of the White House or on the steps of the Capitol building. Local news reporters with sports stories must be standing outside the stadium gate or inside the stadium, amid rows of empty seats.

Reporters providing the word on the stock-market activity on any given day are shown "on the floor" of the exchange. A major highway accident must be visited by a reporter and camera crew— even if the wreckage has been hauled away and all parties involved have moved on—just to say that the news organization was "at the scene." What the director calls "pickup shots" involve videotape of cars driving by.

In truth, stock-market reports could be delivered with just as much accuracy and authority from a television studio, since all relevant market information comes from an electronic display that is visible not only from the trading floor but also from brokers' desktop personal computers in thousands of locations around the United States and thousands more around the world.

101

Obviously it is not necessary to be at the stock exchange to report on the stock market, any more than it is necessary to stand in the middle of a highway to tell about a traffic accident. These are merely examples of the news media's having learned that stories presented with a bit more visual drama attract greater audience attention than stories merely told by a person sitting at a desk. The most obvious way to infuse a feeling of drama into a story or an announcement is to get outside and create a sense of action and immediacy usually absent in a television studio or a newsroom.

There is also the suggestion that a story is more important if it is presented from somewhere—*anywhere*—other than from behind a desk or most other mainstream sites.

The lesson to the publicist in all this is that to attract greater media attention and public interest in a subject, a choice of location can be a chief consideration.

A nonprofessional might think that a subject having news value is enough, but publicists understand the importance of how a subject is "packaged." Part of story packaging is the *photo op.* A visually attractive or interesting setting for an announcement— a garden, the riverbank, a historic landmark, an architecturally important building—is more appealing than a backdrop of a white sheet or a blank wall. And while it seems as if this shouldn't matter, the media are more likely to attend a press conference or a presentation or demonstration if it is held somewhere people would like to go.

Consider: The subject is the announcement of a new real-estate development. Does making the announcement at the site of the proposed development sound more interesting than hearing about it in the conference room of the developer's firm?

The subject is a musical-arts competition for high school students, with prizes of college scholarships. Announce it in the offices of the sponsoring company, or at a site where young people are making music? Obviously, the latter.

A new-product announcement or presentation—or, for that matter, a long-established-product presentation—should be made where the product is manufactured, sold, tested, used, or otherwise displayed.

In situations where going on-site is realistically, physically not possible, a "site" can be created. For example, an Ohio-based maker of hand-care products wants to hold a press conference in New York to announce the launch of a new breakthrough product which is not yet on the market.

One approach, if the company's shares are publicly traded, is to make the announcement from the boardroom of the stock exchange on which the company's shares are listed. Another site might be the community room of a hospital, with a doctor in attendance to say something about skin conditions that will be helped by the product. Other possibilities are a place where the product is likely to be used and where hand care and skin condition are especially important—a beauty salon, health spa, food-service company, jewelry showroom, child-care facility, and so forth. Consider the market for your subject and what possible sites would be appropriate.

Consider, too, that a reason so many press conferences are held at restaurants or private clubs is that, very simply, a good meal with the presentation of information is a reason why some reporters attend one press luncheon or event over another. It may seem silly, and it may not show up on the list of criteria that the best journalism schools provide for *how to decide what the media cover,* but it is a reason nonetheless.

Reporters and editors also know that if they do not attend a given meeting, press conference, luncheon, or speech, a competent publicist who wants his or her subject to be covered will deliver or messenger a copy of the material anyway. So, good food at a nice place is an added incentive or inducement to attract media to an announcement or press conference. While the way to a reporter's heart may not be through his or her stomach, it is often a subtle way to encourage at least coming out to hear a story.

EVENTS AS PUBLICITY SUBJECTS OR VEHICLES

Veteran publicist Jeanette Smith suggests, "Before you decide to stage an event, a full evaluation should be made of why your company or group will have the event. Image—building it, changing it, or softening it—can be all that is needed to justify the decision. A specially created event can be designed to foster and mold a favorable public image for an organization that has been thought of as remote and cold. Any organization can change its image. Perhaps this is the time to consider it, take action, and make the change."

If the objective of your publicity effort is to promote an event, your major issues are the *image and interest level* (or interest *potential*) for the type of event it is, and what *competition* you are facing for attention, interest, support, participation, and/or attendance. Your event may be a one-time-only showing of the Lost Works of Renoir, but if the Rolling Stones Farewell Concert Tour is hitting town that week, don't expect the cover of the Sunday Arts section or the Magazine. The biggest spotlight, at least in theory, goes to the subject with the greatest level of public interest.

Publicists have railed for years about the importance of their subjects over the cover stories that *Time* and *Newsweek* actually choose to run in any given week, but alas, such decisions are either research based or purely subjective. Don't destroy the chance of a good long-term relationship with an editor by protesting your subject's having received less than its fair share of publicity. Take a deep breath, shake your fist at the heavens, and move on.

The basic steps for publicizing an event are the same as those for publicizing a product, cause, company, or candidate: plan and develop your press release, press kit, press conference, interviews and media tour, merchandising program, and follow-up.

What USPs (unique selling points) your event has going for it (celebrity tie-ins, distinguished history or traditions, timely news connection, size or special characteristics of the audience for the event) will help define the message you will use with the media to convince them the event is worthy of publicity. Remember to emphasize *what's in it for the audience.* The media, apart from the trade press and unprincipled tabloids, are far less interested in what you feel you want to accomplish and in what's in it for you.

Your competition for both media and public interest is virtually anything going on at the same time. Despite your uniqueness, covering and/or attending an event very often comes down to what else is happening at the same time. In an era when concerts, fairs, exhibits, lectures, trade shows, sporting events, entertainment, car crashes, market crashes, and myriad other choices are available, the media must decide what to cover most prominently. The public, while aware of an event, must choose whether to attend or not. The publicist would probably prefer that people attend; however, even some events that receive a disappointingly low turnout still achieve and retain a level of public awareness that can and might result in widening the exposure to the event's publicity. More simply, while not attending an event, members of the public know about it and tell others about it, who might in turn tell others. The result—poor attendance but great publicity—could be a short-term setback and a longer-term success.

In some cases the event is not the publicist's main subject, but rather is a vehicle used to help promote the subject. Examples of this are:

- a benefit concert to raise funds for the arts
- a rally or speech to focus attention on an issue or a cause
- a cocktail party to raise campaign funds for a potential candidate
- a dinner with appearances by celebrities as a vehicle to help raise awareness and money for a charity

Publicists find that their work is easier when the subject is a *name*: a person, a place, an issue, a product, or a company that already has public name recognition and/or a core constituency. In such instances the challenges are: getting greater publicity than the competition during the same period, telling the public (and the often jaded media) something it doesn't already know about your subject, and convincing all parties concerned that the publicity is necessary. That is to say, more than a few large, costly projects have sunk because the perception was that a big name was enough to bring people out or that a large constituency for a particular issue or cause could always be counted on to support it with votes or funds.

In publicizing events, whether as a primary subject or as a vehicle developed to help promote a primary subject, there are three stages a publicist must manage. The first is the pre-event, or *advance,* work that will both generate and heighten interest (and perhaps participation); the second is *coverage* once the event is under way; and the third is the *aftermath*: working every possible publicity angle to position the event as successful and exploit the fact that it took place.

Advance work follows the formula as noted (press release, press kit, etc.). The coverage stage will largely reflect how effective your efforts have been in the previous stage. If you have raised the interest level of the event during the first stage, coverage will occur without much effort expended on your part. It is, however, never wise to assume that your good job on phase one will guarantee a good phase two.

Go through a process of sending members of the media personal invitations, VIP passes, guest passes, reserved-seating tickets, press credentials, or a summary schedule or program—and follow it all up with phone calls to confirm, remind, and keep selling until the very end.

After the event, post-event activities can continue for as long as you need them to, with:

- press releases and photos, noting the high points of the events
- newsletters with photographs, highlighting and recapping the event and related or resulting activities (amount of money raised, volunteers recruited, excellent response and commitment from audience, etc.)

- speech transcripts
- a commemorative book
- letters of appreciation to attendees and participants
- letters to the editor, recounting and following through on the message of the event

The after-event period is the time for spinning: putting the best possible look and tone to the event.

SPEECHES

As far as a publicist is concerned, a speech is a great publicity device. The actual speech itself is almost irrelevant. It is what happens before and after the speech that is more important. More people will *hear about* the speech or *read about* it than will actually hear the speech delivered. That's fine. The speaker should be more interested in the message's getting out than in the size of the actual on-site audience.

Publicize the fact that a speech is to be delivered, using all the conventional machinery: letters, postcards, faxes, bulletin boards, calendar notices, newsletter notices, and even—if appropriate to the speaker, subject, and occasion—media alerts. Releasing copies of the full text of the speech to the media, either before or after its presentation, is an optional decision.

Send out a press release noting the highlights or major points of the speech, either before or after, depending on your objectives.

Within 24 hours of the speech, consider issuing a press release reiterating the main points of the text, with a possible comment or two from someone of prominence, in effect, endorsing the points made in reference to the subject of the speech.

Continue to feed follow-up comments about the speech to columnists over the week or two following its delivery.

Are speeches inherently publicity-related events? Unless the speech is to the National Security Council, there is virtually no time when they shouldn't be or couldn't be.

To find the strong points of a speech to publicize, repeat this, by now, familiar exercise: Ask who, what, when, where, why and how.

Who is speaking? Where? Why? About what?

Clearly the location or venue can play a significant role in the ability to maximize publicity relating to a speech; sometimes it's more meaningful than the speaker or the remarks. Someone addressing the American Bar Association, the American Medical Association, the National Rifle Association, the Veterans of Foreign Wars, the League of Women Voters, Greenpeace, or some such notable group will get the media's attention more readily than a speech to the Backyard Club of Lafayette, Indiana.

Nevertheless, the simple reality is that an accountant delivering a lunch-hour speech at a senior citizens center, a lawyer speaking to a law class (or *any* class), and a hospital administrator or a head of sales speaking to a veterans group can all be viable speeches worth publicizing. If a great and prestigious venue can be arranged for the speech, so much the better. But, just as the publicist's role is to *put the best spin* on whatever he or she may have to work with, sometimes it is necessary to, as the technical expression goes, do it with mirrors.

Obviously the subject of the speech itself has a lot to do with choosing and securing a venue for a speech that will work to your advantage in terms of a publicity effort. A group that regards itself as very serious in its purpose—the John Birch Society, for example—will very likely not be inclined to invite a speaker from the entertainment industry or someone who wants to introduce a hair restorative. But, where there's a will and a bit of imagination, some links can be formed.

A catalog from a local college or university will reveal that classes are offered for a diverse range of subjects. Is your message appropriate for any one of these classes? If so, contact the professor and indicate your willingness to have a spokesperson for your subject meet with students before, during, or after class. A press release that summarizes your message and indicates that the subject "addressed a group of university students" has a ring of newsworthiness. It is not necessary to address the entire university population to be quoted as having told university students something of value.

Senior citizens centers, union halls, libraries, singles groups, book groups, stock clubs, churches, and similar such gatherings are appropriate for delivering a speech on social or other issues.

Introducing a new product? Opening a new store? Adding a location? Bringing out a new line of merchandise? Have information to offer that would benefit children or seniors or that speaks to health and safety? Local chambers of commerce or merchants association groups have regular meetings, with committee meetings in between. As with the university audience, while it might be nice, it is not necessary to speak to the entire membership. Delivering a speech to a committee of six people justifies your mailing out reprints to local media or others on your target list, indicating that this is a summary of your remarks to the chamber of commerce committee on new business.

Whatever your subject, it is likely that a local chapter of a trade association would be receptive to your offer to present a well-thought-out talk on a subject the audience would find useful.

In the case of MacNeal Hospital's Women's Health and Wellness Center, the week prior to its official opening was notable for the series of speeches by celebrities not normally expected to be found speaking at a hospital:

- Olympic figure-skating star Dorothy Hamill spoke on women in sports from a health and nutrition perspective.
- Broadway star Chita Rivera spoke on stress-related illnesses common among women in the arts.
- Actress Ann Jillian talked of her experience with breast cancer.
- Gail Sheehy, author of *Passages* and other bestselling books, spoke on health effects of women as they age.

It must be noted that these celebrities were paid speaking fees for their participation and that the total cost for a week of high-visibility activities was substantial, relative to the hospital's usually modest budget for marketing. But the hospital was more than satisfied with the resulting publicity. The facility and the issue of women's health were given great prominence, in no way overshadowed by the presence of well-known personalities.

The subject of women's health is one that can be presented to editors and producers almost any time and be considered timely and worthy of consideration. But why *your* health facility? And why *now*? How do you relate the subject to your interests? One way is your unique selling points; another might be the presence of well-known people delivering speeches as a drawing card.

BENEFITS, PARTIES, AND RECEPTIONS

Truman Capote defined the last years of his life not by writing as much as by throwing lavish parties. Irving "Swifty" Lazar was known as one of the most powerful of agents, negotiating multi-million-dollar contracts for, among others, Johnny Carson and Richard Nixon; yet, people who knew him remember him best for his parties following the Academy Awards—the most sought-after invitation in town. Consider how many of the best-known public figures are known, in large part, from the newspaper and magazine photos and TV news images of them entering or leaving a party.

Benefits, parties, and receptions are publicity vehicles. They are see-and-be-seen venues that, while raising money for worthy causes and candidates or honoring individuals, are ultimately photo opportunities and column items.

Underwriting a benefit can be costly, as publicity efforts go. A well-attended formal dinner party, with at the very least a professional master of ceremonies and very likely entertainment and music, at an appropriate hotel ballroom or comparable facility, typically has a visible correlation among its cost, its degree of lavishness, and the amount of publicity it generates.

Many corporations engaged in "cause marketing"—supporting and funding social causes or charitable ventures—anchor such efforts with an annual dinner to honor someone or as a forum for speech making. Such designated functions serve to focus attention on the sponsor's or underwriter's participation, and much of the media find events such as these difficult to ignore due to the worthiness of their purpose, as well as their visual interest.

Press Conferences

The most commonly offered advice to publicists regarding press conferences is to not have them.

A majority of press conferences occur in movies, where it appears all news is made in about a half hour and the entire press corps gathers in one room and waits for the announcement that will have enormous implications.

In real life the White House, Congress, and the Pentagon have daily press briefings, and the rest of the world pretty much communicates with the media through press releases, faxes, E-mail, and telephone calls. There *are* in fact a vast number of press conferences called each year, most of which are viewed by reporters and editors as self-aggrandizing and very light on news.

The demands on reporters' time are such that, in order to justify leaving the newsroom for what amounts to a couple of hours at least, and attending a press conference, the payback had better be worth it. Usually it's not.

One factor that holds down press conference attendance is that editors and reporters know that if they ask the publicist for a copy of the press release and other material being distributed at the press conference, it will be supplied immediately. The reporter who stays at his or her desk, choosing to skip the conference, can ask what went on there, receive a briefing, and know as much as if he or she had attended. The publicist may be annoyed that the reporter was a no-show, but the publicist's greater concern is that the media give attention to the subject. In that regard, the publicist doesn't care if the reporter slept through the press conference, just as long as the story gets in the paper or on TV.

Celebrities call press conferences. Businesses and individuals who are the subjects of a scandal or are involved in an investigation or a major legal action will call a press conference to speak to all reporters at once, rather than one at a time in phone conversations. In such instances the idea of a press conference seems like a good one. It does, after all, put the official statement on the record for everyone to hear at the same time.

Good reporters, however, follow up privately, so the press conference really doesn't work as a means of eliminating individual questions and pursuit. Moreover, reporters don't like to ask their best questions in the presence of other reporters.

It is also a fact of life today that people don't want to answer a reporter's toughest questions, and this is the type of exchange that a reporter—as well as a subject or spokesperson—would prefer to have in private or over the phone.

The presence of a celebrity, a demonstration of a new product, or an announcement of a merger or joint venture, for which all participants are present for questioning at a press conference, can add sizzle to the event.

A downside consideration of press conferences is their interactive nature. That is, after an absolutely great presentation during which things couldn't go better, a reporter asks a question that could be embarrassing or to which the speaker doesn't have an answer. Another questioner, inspired or emboldened, picks up the thread and asks a follow-up question, with the same result. The perfect press conference to introduce or promote a subject has taken a wrong turn.

Some people, it must be said, thrive under such circumstances. Presidents Kennedy and Clinton are examples of men who can operate at the top of their form when an unexpectedly tough or dicey question is put to them. Their responses, showing a quick mind and a solid command of facts, often are the high points of such sessions.

But most people are not John F. Kennedy or Bill Clinton when it comes to press conferences or to interacting with the media. Is it necessary to put a subject—a CEO or other spokesperson—in such a potentially vulnerable position?

It might be assumed that in a typical press conference to cut a ribbon for a new community hospital wing, announce a school building plan, dedicate a mall, bring out a new dog-food line, or launch a fund-raising campaign, tough questions—or rudeness on the part of the attending media—would be unlikely. Maybe, but maybe not. A press conference, as any other action that asks people to take notice of something, must be viewed with consideration to a "worst-case" scenario.

It has been noted that some publicists like trying to lure reporters out to an event or a presentation with the promise of a good meal from a trendy restaurant. A press conference should be well planned and respectful of the media's time. Most are not, and members of the media regard them with irritation, despite the fact that many publicists think attending press conferences is only part of the reporter's job. In a perfect world, perhaps everyone would perform what other people thought of as their jobs with a spring in their steps and a smile. But, as publicists need the cooperation, support, and goodwill of the media to carry their messages, they are well advised to keep antagonistic behavior to a minimum.

Is there a more effective alternative to a press conference? Can the same objective be accomplished in less time and less cost—and with less exposure to negative reaction—with a press release, a photo release, and a few well-chosen follow-up phone calls to selected reporters? Such questions should be raised and considered before you ask a reporter to drop everything and come out to hear what you have to say.

INTERVIEWS

Publicists should think of interviews on two levels. The first is the publicist interviewing people within the company, association, organization, or client group—whatever the subject entity of the publicity effort—for material. It is not unusual for a CEO to engage the services of a publicist to help the company become better known, and the publicist sets out, only to find the folks within the organization somewhere between apathetic and outright closed-mouthed on the subject of what the company is doing that is newsworthy. The publicist could hang around the water cooler, hoping to overhear something interesting, or start at the top of the organization chart and begin interviewing officers, department heads, managers, or principals of the operation.

Suddenly "What's new?" becomes a serious question that needs an answer. People very close to a subject are often inclined to overlook aspects that are interesting or noteworthy to outsiders.

New products, improved products, an extension of a product (a new size or flavor, or an alternative such as a "light" version or seasonal adaptation), a new executive, a new board member, a staff addition or promotion from within, a new promotional campaign in the sales area, a new service added for the benefit of customers or clients or the organization staff (anything from one-day delivery to on-site day care), new company or product graphics, a new regional office or satellite location, modernization of facilities or outsourcing of functions, a new acquisition or upgrading of systems—all are examples of noteworthy occurrences and issues within a typical company or organization.

Sometimes what's *old* becomes story material. An employee marking a major milestone with the organization, a celebration of many years at the same location, the noteworthy anniversary of a customer or client—a person or company representing a long and valued relationship—are all possible subjects for publicity.

The second type of interview is the one most people think of first, the one in which Barbara Walters or Larry King asks the questions that define the subject as important.

OK, perhaps most subjects don't get to *start* with Barbara or Larry. For most, it's a get-acquainted interview with the local daily or weekly paper or radio station. But in the age of modern media, it is not unusual or unrealistic for a well-written press release on a subject of value to earn follow-up questions from the *Wall Street Journal* or CNN. The media are looking for new subjects, new approaches to consistently popular subjects, and new sources to interview about them.

When such calls come, you might not have time to prepare a response, so allow for the fact that, if your story is a good one and is well presented in your press release, media alert, position paper, or initial phone call to media representatives, questions might be forthcoming from media at any and all levels of the spectrum.

Be prepared. If possible, have information available that elaborates on your position as stated in your release. At the very least, be prepared to offer additional comments orally.

A publicist should always put himself or herself in the reporter's position, both when preparing the initial material and in preparing responses to follow-up questions. Consider what are the most likely questions and requests for information, and have the material ready, in writing if possible, to give to a reporter or to read.

Be concise. Reporters may ask for elaboration on a particular point, but if they don't ask, make certain that your response effectively addresses the subject as you would like to see it represented.

In an in-person interview, the subject of the interview must be conscious of gestures, mannerisms, and body language. Reporters often will note that someone "appeared uneasy" or "seemed nervous." The following actions will help ensure success:

- Be prepared. Preparation makes you feel more confident, and that comes through in the interview.

- Look the way you want to look. If you want a more executive or authoritative look, wear a jacket. For a more "working" feeling: coat off, tie loose, perhaps sleeves rolled up slightly for men; business casual for women, perhaps with a jacket draped over the back of a chair; papers and open books in view.
- Know the interviewer. Be familiar with (having at least looked over) some of the interviewer's work.
- Be friendly but businesslike. The interviewer is judging you on your professionalism.
- Open interviews with a succinct, useful prepared statement to help you set the tone and take control of the session.
- Don't swear. It seems as if this shouldn't have to be said, but given the steady drift to more crude conversation in public, it bears mentioning. Swearing may be socially more acceptable in adult conversation than it was a few years ago, but it might very likely seem more offensive than down-to-earth.
- Don't smoke. Some people think it conveys a particular image, and it does—but it might not be the image that will serve your purpose. Don't take the chance.
- Stay calm; make eye contact; choose your words carefully; stay with the points you want to make.
- If you don't understand an interviewer's question, ask that it be rephrased. If a reporter attempts to interpret your comments by suggesting, "In other words, you are saying . . . ," unless it is a vast and positive improvement on your own choice of expression, do not be intimidated or reluctant to simply say that you would prefer to be quoted in your own words.
- *Never* go "off the record." An apology or even a written retraction can never undo damage from a misstated or misunderstood reference that probably never should have been made in the first place.

- Keep interviews to less than one hour. If they go longer, people tend to repeat themselves, and their minds wander.
- Remember political correctness, but don't overdo it, since the essence of "pc" is really just good manners. An operative point is that people may not feel as you do about certain subjects, and it can be a mistake to assume that they do and get too familiar. Don't get too personal.
- Offer to be available for a follow-up phone conversation if necessary.

Overwhelmingly reporters are reasonable, ethical, and friendly, but in an age of such intense media competition and a desire for the most colorful quotes, an interview subject must be advised to be guarded. One cannot ever assume that a reporter has the subject's best interests at heart. The more dramatic and colorful a story appears to be, the better it is for the reporter, not necessarily for the subject.

When the call comes from a tabloid show—*60 Minutes, Dateline, Inside Edition*—it's probably a good idea to be vacationing on another planet. Some media like to focus on the more sensational, more exploitive, or darker side of a subject. Seriously, then, when put in a position of having to respond to calls from tabloid media:

1. Don't try to win them over with your charm.
2. Don't try to outsmart them by confronting them aggressively and acting like the arrogant TV lawyers most people dislike.
3. Don't try to outrun them. A camera lingering on your rear end, in most cases, doesn't present you at your best.

Take a deep breath, offer a prepared statement in writing, and decline on-camera conversation. People rarely come off well in these situations; the best you can hope for is damage control and minimal losses.

The Internet

Getting attention can be tough in any medium, but on the Internet, your audience really has to come looking for you.

Is it just a big electronic phone directory? Or a catalog or a video game? Or is it the access route to an unlimited store of information? Or the information itself? The answer, of course, is yes.

The Internet is the greatest, broadest, and most fertile field of virtually unlimited opportunities, and at the same time, it is a potential minefield.

Not many years ago, *the Internet, the World Wide Web,* and *cyberspace* were terms that did not exist. Today they exist in a major way. By the time you finish reading this sentence, what all is encompassed by these terms may very well have changed. However, keeping up with technological advancements in communication is surprisingly easy. Daily newspapers, magazines, and television have accepted the fact that an apparent revolution is under way and accord both the phenomenon itself and its many uses considerable ongoing coverage.

Newsletters, magazines, bulletin boards, chat rooms, and volumes of minutiae now line the information superhighway. The Internet has evolved—and is still evolving—to span an extremely broad range for:

- news
- entertainment
- education
- interactive communication
- financial data

To publicists this reality represents the best of times and the worst of times.

An almost unimaginably broad range of positions exists where a publicist might place a press release, a bio, a profile, a speech, brochure text with graphics, or an entire book-length file with all an audience could ever want to know about a subject. It is also where pranksters and villains have placed bogus press releases and articles and phony quotes and has proved to be a showcase of many new publications that are totally without credibility. The sophistication of the technology makes "spoofsites" virtually indistinguishable from legitimate sites.

Almost every legitimate newspaper and magazine—*Time, Newsweek,* the *Chicago Tribune,* the *New York Times,* the *Wall Street Journal,* the *Washington Post, Fortune, Playboy,* and countless others—is on "the Web" with expanded versions of its established print products. The World Wide Web is a long list of publications, catalogs, brochures, ads, programs, and party lines.

Kathryn Coombs, cofounder of Washington Webworks, creates websites for candidates and members of Congress. She notes that much of the attraction of the World Wide Web is in its cost effectiveness, where you can create a high-quality glossy message on the Internet "for the paper-clip budget of a traditional advertising campaign—under $50,000."

The World Web Shopper promotes itself as "the most user-friendly shopping mall on the net."

In the most dramatic reflection of the phrase "If you can't beat 'em, join 'em" are the television networks, such as ABC, CBS, and NBC, which would—and did—consider the Internet competition for the most demographically desirable audience. These TV networks have created websites which they, in turn, promote ceaselessly on their network television programs.

"Want to know more about the program you just saw? Check out our website."

Want to talk to the performer, producer, or politician you just saw on a TV show? Go to the Web. It is increasingly common for TV and print ads, as well as for programming and news material, to be followed by a website address, presumably so that the people who didn't want something to end will get their way.

MSNBC, a cable-TV joint venture of Microsoft and the National Broadcasting Company, encourages viewers to comment and "become part of the television program" via the Internet. CNN too includes information it receives via E-mail in much of its programming.

It might just look like a huge media amusement park, except for the tens of thousands of website owners that *aren't* media names. Your favorite musical performer, your favorite breakfast cereal, catalogs, department stores, bookstores, brokerage firms, major stock exchanges, hundreds of politicians, and the Pope all have their own websites. It doesn't get more respectable than that.

Some marketers have expressed concern that the Internet "audience" tends to be slightly elitist. Obviously, not everyone is either computer literate or computer inclined, and those who sit at their PCs, browsing or surfing the net, do believe they have access to so much that they are literally plugged in to the world.

Much of what appears on the Internet has the look of credibility—that is, it appears very much like material presented by major publications, such as *Time* or *Newsweek*—but in fact may be the work of a single individual who is far from what the industry has ever recognized as a "publisher." This situation has caused problems on occasion.

No less a respected and respectable public figure than the former presidential press secretary Pierre Salinger quoted an item that appeared on the Internet, treating the reference as if it had the weight of legendary fact-checkers from *The New Yorker* magazine behind it. What Salinger quoted was a rumor. What resulted was confusion and months of disparaging references from news reporters, and more than a few gags in comedians' monologues. The incident proved to be a major blow to the gentleman's public image.

The Free Press in the Age of Technology offers this insight: "Imagine a scenario in which anyone could pretend to be a journalist and journalists were under no obligation to check their facts or to make sure that what they were reporting was true. Imagine the Internet being used as a vehicle to introduce a potentially dangerous product, reporting results of a survey that in fact doesn't exist, or offer performance claims for a product or service without having to actually document the claims. All are as close as your modem."

The fact is that a subject not having its own website today is a cause for suspicion. Reporters, editors, and producers, already "online" all day anyway, routinely check the Web for information about a subject before calling with their first question.

The net is interactive while also allowing an individual or a business to be on only one side of it—either as the consumer or the supplier of information—or both.

It would seem that a publicist would be remiss in not putting a press release on the Internet, much as he or she might put the same release on a newswire.

It would also seem that, in order to be taken seriously, a subject must have its own page. The fact that visiting a website address published in a magazine ad brings the audience little more than another viewing of the same ad indicates that people have indeed concluded that having a website is the thing to do . . . so, now what? If a company or enterprise has trouble filling a four-page newsletter with interesting material several times a year, keeping an updated website could be a challenge, to say the least. Often newspapers and magazines will be given a "column item" about something new, interesting, or of value on the Internet. Servicing the media with such modest items is an excellent way of helping to build interest in the site. It is, however, important that there be enough on the site that the item alone doesn't appear more informational than the source from which it was extracted.

It has become more and more common for both members of the general public and the media to check the net for a subject, much the way they used to check phone books or any number of professional directories. It is for this reason, basically to remain competitive, that websites have been set up by enterprises that one might otherwise be surprised to see promoted on the net, such as supermarkets, drugstores, furniture stores, auto dealers, tire stores, and churches.

The *Chicago Tribune,* for example, carries a weekly (paid) "Internet Directory A to Z." On a typical day, one might find the Internet listings of the *Tribune* itself, directing readers to the range of information services available from its website; chiropractic centers; health-care services; catering; real estate; jewelry; printing; and pizza. Many of the listings, not surprisingly, are from enterprises offering to create websites and market on the Internet. Agencies that once prospected so aggressively for new clients now find a large fertile pool of businesses unfamiliar with the Internet and wondering how to use this new means of reaching out to the universe.

An entire culture exists that relates to few other avenues of communication as strongly—almost passionately—as it does to the Internet. If this is the target audience for your message, then clearly your publicity effort must be heavily built around use of the net. If, on the other hand, your best profile of your constituency does not suggest a significant demographic overlap with Internet users, focusing on more traditional media would be more advisable.

The day may well come, as some people believe, when the personal computer, linked to the Internet, will replace the telephone, television, direct mail, and all manner of print media. For some people, this day has already arrived. Overwhelmingly, however, websites must still compete for audience attention in the same way other media do: using TV, radio, mail, outdoor, and print to direct the audience to the offerer's location. With this in mind, include the Internet on your media list with bulletin boards, home pages, and listings of as many places as your audience might be. But don't neglect the mainstream media which, though they may lose a bit of their luster amid the high-tech innovations, still are where the greatest audience turns for information.

AT A GLANCE
CREATING OPPORTUNITIES

- Having a reporter "on the scene" is a point of competitive consideration with most media.

- An obvious way to infuse drama and to make a story more "visual" for TV and photo purposes is to choose a dramatic location.

- The choice of a location for an announcement or an event is extremely important. While the value inherent in the story itself should be enough, the overall "packaging" can make an enormous difference in how successful the effort will be.

- A riverbank, a landmark building, a historical site, or a place of architectural interest can provide a great backdrop to an announcement or an event.

- To the degree that it is possible, make the site relevant to the subject. In a general sense, popular or trendy restaurants are a good place for an announcement or an event because of the "halo effect," or identification with the positive image of the place.

- What determines the attendance, and potentially the success of your event, are the subject's image, the level of interest in the subject, and what events are competing for attention at the same time.

continued

- In your presentation, always emphasize the advantages to your public of what you have to offer.

- If a publicity program for an event is effective, people—whether they can attend the event or not—tell other people who tell other people about it.

- While events may be the singular subject of a publicity effort, they may also be vehicles for other subjects, such as with concerts, dinners, parties, tributes, awards ceremonies, rallies, or speeches for charity.

- The three stages of event publicity are the *advance, coverage,* and *aftermath.*

- Speeches are also either events unto themselves or merely vehicles to promote a subject, wherein the coverage of the speech is more important than the speech itself.

- The location (or venue) where the speech is delivered can lend added importance or credibility to the subject (a university, a medical center, a day care center, etc.).

- Benefits, parties, and receptions are excellent publicity vehicles.

- Reporters tend to view most press conferences as light on news and largely unnecessary.

- The presence of a celebrity and/or a choice location will boost interest and attendance at a press conference.

continued

- While a press conference requires a performance, remember the role of the audience, and be prepared for the tough or rude question.

- Internal interviews are a way of keeping up on what is going on within a company that may have publicity potential.

- In developing ideas for publicity programs, it's fine to be on the lookout for what's new, but do not overlook what's old. An old and valued employee, a long time at the same location, or status as the market leader (most imitated) are valid ideas as well.

- Prepare for an interview as for a speech or a media appearance. Be prepared, look good, speak thoughtfully and concisely, be confident, and be mindful of body language and gestures that might be misinterpreted.

- Never go "off the record" in an interview. The classic phrase may sound good, but it has caused a lot of grief.

- Getting positive attention is always tough, but on the Internet especially, your audience has to really want to find you.

- The Internet is a fertile field of opportunities for publicists, but it can also be a minefield.

- Beware of "spoofsites": phony press releases and other bogus information on the Internet which can create a less than positive environment for your message.

continued

- An entire culture now exists that relates better to the Internet than to any other media.

- Don't expect more from the Internet than it can deliver. Use it as a component of your media plan, but continue to focus attention on more mainstream, traditional means to get your message across. As your program matures, put greater emphasis on the media segment that has produced the best response.

5

Great Expectations

To generate publicity, to get your message out to the largest audience in the shortest time, you need to take advantage of the media opportunities available. You have carefully defined your target audience, discriminatingly identified your target media, and developed your basic materials to conform to the highest professional standards: press release, press kit, backgrounders, bios, and fact sheets are ready for presentation. Reaching out to make contact with the media is the next critical step in the process and one that is often intimidating. What if what you offer is rejected? What if there is a total absence of interest in your subject? What if you worked hard planning the picnic and it rains?

It could happen. Anything can happen. Successful publicity campaigns are the result of good planning, good execution, and good luck.

If you have effectively performed the planning steps, you have focused your message and narrowed your list so that the people you will be approaching will be somewhere between receptive and interested in your subject. You are not calling entertainment reporters with technology stories, or business editors with science stories. The reporters, editors, and producers you call should have an assigned or established interest in your subject. It may be the reporter's "beat" or a subject the reporter has written on more than once.

Whether you are an experienced publicist or someone in an organization who has been assigned to manage the publicity effort, just sending out material alone is rarely enough to generate interest. *The media must be called, often several times—both before and after material has been sent.* It is the call that brings attention to the press release or kit and very often determines whether the material is used, filed, ignored, or tossed. The *quality* of coverage is also directly related to the follow-up calls.

If you are unfamiliar with the reporter you are calling, be professional and well organized but not *mechanized.* You are a publicist—a news and information source—not a telephone solicitor.

The most successful media relationships are based on mutual trust and on the reporter's, editor's, or producer's knowing that the publicist will show respect for his or her time and deadlines, be honest, and handle the presentation of information quickly, accurately, and with integrity.

A publicist has to be convinced of the value of his or her own message and then convince others of that value, often one reporter at a time.

WRITING IT RIGHT

Sometimes, particularly in large public relations firms, staff writers will prepare the press releases, fact sheets, and backgrounders that the publicists then present. If this system is effective for you or your organization, then keep doing it that way. But a publicist is generally better equipped to present a message that he or she has had a hand in crafting. Publicists are communicators, and writing is a communication skill.

Some publicists will claim they are not writers—that they *can't* write. It may very well be true that not everyone can write, but to repeat: publicists are communicators, and writing is a communication skill. It is not necessary for the publicist to outdo Jane Austen or Henry James. The most effective publicity material should not read as if it were a novel or an ad, but as if it were a news story. Not to take anything away from veteran news writers, but presenting the facts—who, what, when, where, why, and how—is a pretty straightforward process that can be accomplished usually with six declarative sentences. Adding a bit of color, style, or sizzle is fine—even appropriate—but reporters and editors don't want to read press releases that wax poetic without providing the necessary facts, and they certainly don't demand more than that.

In creating good working relationships with reporters, editors, and producers, it is useful to the publicist to display his or her competency on occasion and to be known for having good communication skills, being knowledgeable on the relevant subjects, and perhaps even being "a good writer."

James Kirkwood was a novelist and Pulitzer Prize–winning playwright. When asked how he dealt with "writer's block"—feeling that you just can't find the words that convey what you want to communicate—he said he thought the problem was often one of trying too hard. He said that when he was stuck for the perfect phrase, he would stop demanding it. He would fantasize that someone appeared in his doorway and asked him what it was he was trying to say.

Kirkwood would explain to his imaginary guest what he was trying to say. By his verbalizing it as if responding to a question, the essential facts of what he wanted to say would come through. He would get it down on paper just that way and then go back and edit it, stylizing and modifying. Essentially, his point was that *how* you say something can be refined in the editing, but *that* you say something is what gets the job done. Just getting the essence of what you need and want to say on paper is getting you most of the way there.

RESPONDING TO MEDIA INQUIRIES

Remember when you are speaking with the media that not only are you speaking for your subject company, product, business, or client, but also you may be the *only* person speaking for that subject, and the image and attitude you convey may well be the only impression the reporter will get of the subject.

In most instances, members of the media calling for information or clarification will be courteous, friendly, and professional. There are times, of course, when this will not be the case. A reporter who has been transferred from person to person, or has been left "on hold" for a period of time, may be annoyed or exasperated and may reflect these feelings in conversation with you. On the other hand, the reporter may be, by temperament or affectation, rude or abrupt. Be prepared for either possibility.

Then . . . relax. It is easy to understand why some people feel uncomfortable or even intimidated when speaking with a member of the press, expecting that their remarks will be reported in print and attributed to them.

If you know, or expect, that a reporter will be calling and have the luxury of any advance preparation time, write down several brief, concise, factual points to which you will want to be sure to refer once the conversation is under way.

It is appropriate for reporters to call with questions, but the reporter's desire to speak with you does not take precedence over other needs or responsibilities of the moment.

When responding to media queries, keep these points in mind:

- If the reporter calls at an inconvenient time, or you feel ill prepared to respond to inquiries, ask if you can call back or if the reporter can call you at a later predetermined time. If that is not possible, tell the reporter that you will try to have an associate return the call as soon as possible.
- Media deadlines are not flexible. If it is necessary to return a reporter's call, do it promptly, or have an associate call back promptly to arrange a mutually convenient time for the reporter to talk with you. To not return a call promptly (or at all) sends a message that you are unresponsive—and perhaps deliberately so. This is not usually reflected positively in the reporter's story.

- Be professional; choose your words carefully; avoid appearing glib; respond to the reporter's questions as you might to questions from your boss, a shareholder in your company or project, or a professional associate.
- People hear things differently and often remember things differently. Take notes during your conversation, and keep a summary record of any factual information you provided.
- Wait for the reporter's questions; do not volunteer information or attempt to lead or direct the conversation. Sometimes an experienced publicist can do this, especially one who is acquainted with the reporter, but reporters want to feel that they are conducting their own interviews and not being "fed" what they didn't come looking for.
- Do not address subjects or questions outside of your own area of responsibility or expertise. If necessary, offer to call back once you've been briefed on the relevant data.
- Answer questions as briefly and directly as possible. Reporters are normally either taking notes or recording the conversation. The more concise your answer, the more likely it is to be used in the story.
- Consider if any authoritative or printed information exists that addresses the reporter's questions or the specific subject of the conversation or interview. If possible, offer to provide the information (by fax) as a means of being helpful and forthcoming and of making sure that the information is accurate.
- It is perfectly appropriate to tell a reporter that a specific piece of information requested is privileged or proprietary information and that you are not at liberty to provide it.
- Avoid offering anecdotes that may inadvertently reveal privileged or proprietary information or take the interview off-track.
- Never go "off the record" with a reporter. While the phrase has always sounded good in the movies, it is often subject

to misinterpretation. If you do not want to see something in print, don't say it.

- At the conclusion of the conversation, report it to appropriate persons within your organization. Review your notes of the conversation, and if appropriate, call the reporter back as soon as possible with any additional factual information that may be relevant.

WORKING WITH VOLUNTEERS AND COMMITTEES

Many organizations, such as schools, hospitals, and political campaigns, rely heavily on the use of volunteers. Understandably, when people are not being paid for their services, they may feel that they deserve special consideration, recognition, respect, and certainly appreciation. To schedule a recognition ceremony, luncheon, or other function and present certificates, pins, or other mementos is appropriate and encourages both goodwill and better productivity. Everyone likes to feel appreciated.

Usually the more volunteers an organization has, the smaller its budget. Sometimes these unpaid, dedicated people are among the rank-and-file of a company, a civic or social cause, or a campaign; in other instances, as in the case of the publicity committee of a professional association, they may be highly experienced, competitive, skilled communicators. In either instance, the challenge is to keep everyone focused and get the most from the talent and resources available.

Committees, boards, and volunteer armies are a great source of ideas. "Brainstorming" sessions that encourage everyone to be involved can produce innovative approaches to publicizing a message, as well as a potentially wider range of contacts with relationships and access to suppliers, vendors, and . . . more volunteers.

As in any organized situation, assignments must be clear to avoid overlapping functions and to be certain each participant knows his or her role. Publicity efforts at all levels have similar requirements: writers, photographers, sign painters, typists, copiers,

envelope stuffers, kit packers, drivers, escorts, and so on. And in
cases in which funds are not available to pay mailing services, telemarketers, handbill distributors, cooks, waiters, and others, volunteers may save the day.

Few political campaigns at either the local or national level
could likely succeed without volunteers who largely perform functions directed by publicists, such as distributing literature; making
phone calls; and attending or hosting luncheons, breakfasts, dinners, coffee breaks, parties, and backyard gatherings, presenting the
candidate's best image and getting the message out to the local
media and the community.

Similarly, local school functions—usually fund-raisers, from
fun fairs to concerts—depend on volunteer armies, the largest contingent of which are engaged in some publicity-related efforts to
promote; recruit sponsors, underwriters, and donors; and manage
the event. As stated earlier, volunteers are important to a publicity
campaign, but just as important are the opportunities created by
events to honor volunteers.

WHAT THINGS COST

Publicity is one of the most cost-efficient components of a marketing or public relations program, but it is not cost free. Whether personnel are on staff or freelance, there is the publicist's fee and
photographer's fee, and even with help from volunteers, the most
modest publicity program needs press releases, press kits, and informational literature. This means printing costs and, more than likely,
postage, messenger, and shipping fees. Sending the members of the
media a fax may be cheaper than a messenger service, but it still
means telephone charges, supplies, and purchase or rental of the
equipment: copiers, fax machines, and word processors just to start.

The answer to what a publicity program should cost is that
there is no one price or standard formula. Each campaign or ongoing program must be based on addressing its own specific objectives.
There are, however, methods of keeping costs down:

- Are there strategies and tactics in your plan that can be carried out by volunteers instead of by paid staff?
- Are there potential "partners" who can be brought into your effort and share costs or can provide certain machinery that can be utilized at little or no cost, such as video capabilities, creating websites, or making office and/or meeting space available?
- Can student interns be used in some capacity in exchange for school credit?

Typically a publicist will amass a pile of press clippings that resulted from his or her efforts, measure the size of the stories—including photos—and calculate how much that same space would have cost had it been purchased at prevailing ad rates. Then, looking at the total dollar outlay for the publicity effort, the publicist will compare the two, suggesting that publicity brought the subject exposure and visibility at a fraction of the price of advertising. Of course, even the publicist knows that isn't a totally fair comparison.

Nonetheless, to prepare a budget for publicity, some companies use a rule that between 5 percent and 15 percent of the company's advertising budget gets earmarked for publicity. If the company or organization is not an advertiser, another approach is to contact public relations firms that might be interested in handling your subject as an account and ask what they would charge as a monthly retainer (as opposed to charges for a specific project). Calculate the average of the agencies' estimated monthly fees, add projected expenses, and you have an estimated budget figure. Even if you do not retain the services of an agency, it is unlikely you could match their services less expensively in-house.

RIDE SHARING: CO-OP PROGRAMS AND PUBLICITY PARTNERS

In co-op advertising, a manufacturer might create a great-looking ad that cost, perhaps, many thousands of dollars and offer it to a local retailer or distributor or other commercial entity to list its name, address, and phone number and place in a local paper. Sometimes the manufacturer will even pay all or part of the media placement costs, or simply offer to reimburse the business for a specific amount or percentage of the costs to advertise the manufacturer's product locally.

Co-op publicity works a lot the same way. Two entities with a common objective find a way to cooperate, thereby hopefully reducing the cost to one or both of the parties and creating results that benefit both. Sometimes the deal is arranged and obvious, such as the local McDonald's donating food to a charity auction. Both the charity and McDonald's are interested in publicity for their own enterprises, and while neither may mention the other, it is clear that they are both there and *why* they are there.

Sometimes co-op publicity occurs unintentionally, as in the case of former Chrysler chairman Lee Iacocca appearing in ads for his company's products while wearing his raincoat with the readily identifiable Burberry lining clearly displayed. It was a great free plug for Burberry, identifying it as the choice of a high-powered CEO, while asserting the CEO's discriminating taste in clothing.

Other examples of co-op publicity include:

• Jeweler Harry Winston routinely loans pieces of fine jewelry to celebrities to wear to the Academy Awards ceremonies, with the understanding that this information will be provided to the media. The celebrities never mention it directly, as they are concerned with publicizing their films or other projects or merely themselves. The Harry Winston jewels go along for a well-photographed, publicized ride.

• Sponsors of U.S. Olympic athletes will pay to have their names and logos identified with the games and the athletes, but very often the audience will hear the athlete's personal trainers discussed or the name and location of the gym or other facility where the athletes prepare. Or the athletes will be photographed or shown on television, sipping a Gatorade (which had been provided at no charge). These are neither *cross-sells* nor *product placements,* in advertising parlance. They are names that have been identified and publicized as associated with another subject entity. In that way, they are not only associated, but also publicity partners: whenever one is referenced, the image of the other is likely to appear as well.

• A commentator or columnist describing a newsworthy occurrence, meeting, or press conference may mention that the scene was the Palmer House Hilton hotel. The name of the hotel is irrelevant to the story, but the mention nonetheless is not just publicity for the hotel, but a *positioning* form of publicity that identifies the hotel with an event of particular importance, excitement, or glamour.

• The band appeared on network television and concert stages coast to coast, and each time they did, the name *Ludwig* was clearly visible on the drums, *Gibson* on each guitar, and *Yamaha* on the electric keyboard. The audience was not aware that the instruments had been provided free of charge in exchange for assurance that the brand names would not be covered over.

• The popular columnist and television news commentator would often gesture with a pen in his hand—the same pen that was pictured in his hand on the covers of at least two books. The white star on the shiny black pen clearly identified it as a rather pricey Mont Blanc and identified the man as someone of discrimination, with an appreciation for fine, very expensive pens. The same impression of the man would not have been suggested had the pen in his hand been a 49-cent Bic.

• Lapel pins have long been both a decorative element and a symbol of pride and community among members of unions, fraternities, and numerous religious sects and denominations. In recent times, lapel "symbols" have been devised to publicize various causes: red ribbons to bring attention to the need for AIDS research; white ribbons to promote breast cancer awareness; Olympics insignia pins identifying sports fans; specific sports and team pins . . . These items are typically available from merchants and service organizations that wish to identify themselves with these causes, events, and campaigns.

• Over the years, a number of restaurants have introduced a small "heart" symbol next to certain menu entries, with a footnote explaining that the American Heart Association has designated these meals as "heart healthy." This service to health-conscious diners also raises the exposure and recognition of the American Heart Association as the credible authority on such subjects.

• For at least two generations products have carried the *Good Housekeeping* Seal of Approval, a recognized symbol of adherence to high quality standards—and a plug for *Good Housekeeping* magazine.

• The Harvard Classics is a 50-volume set of great books. These books have nothing to do with Harvard University, yet it is impossible for a reader or observer to view the cover or spine of a fine copy of any one of these books—or the ads or literature used to promote them—without flashing, however briefly, on Harvard University, long regarded as a symbol of excellence in education. In this way the books and the university, unrelated as they are, have become partners in publicity.

CREATING CREDIBILITY

The American Tobacco Company is what its name says it is, and any message it might present will be colored by that accordingly. But the *Institute for Tobacco Research and Study* implies an entity devoted to education, research, and potentially a significant diversity of opinion on concerns ranging from big issues to minutiae. But is that so? The answer depends on whom you ask.

The tobacco industry says the *Institute* is a "think tank" in which distinguished persons review and analyze data from the serious to the suspect in a search for fair and unbiased conclusions. Critics of the industry say the *Institute* is little more than a public relations front, funded by big tobacco in an attempt to lend a semblance of respectability to those interests that, separately and together, represent an industry deservedly under attack.

Whew!

Strong stuff. And then there is the *Alliance for Smokers' Rights.*

Right.

But between the tobacco companies and their critics is the public. What does the public think? While there is a range of opinion, the fact is that the public—and the media—still show a high degree of respect for entities that profess to align themselves with education and research. Such organizations appear to be created for noble purposes, even when they have their critics.

Enter the *Institute.*

Many publicists believe that to get the attention of the media, a lofty purpose and a name to go with it can be very helpful.

In such a spirit, it can be noted that on most days both National Public Radio (NPR) and television's C-Span will feature interviews with spokespersons from such formidable (or not) entities as the *Citizens Action Council,* the *Public Policy Institute,* or *Friends of the Library.* The humblest of these organizations can *sound* impressive to much of the audience, even if the organization consists only of its "executive director" and a telephone answering machine.

The *National Legal and Policy Center* is essentially a spokesgroup of the Republican party, well represented on major and minor news and talk shows. If the host were to announce the guest as a Republican spokesperson, the guest's bias would be clear and his or her comments filtered, and even possibly dismissed, by a segment of the audience that would reject partisan views. But by being from the *National Legal and Policy Center,* the guest appears to be a lofty intellectual of high purpose—objective, nonpartisan, and authoritative. Spokespersons present the same message in the same words, but as the packages are different, one gets an open-minded hearing while the other gets taken with a grain of salt.

For the added ring of authority, some special interests have been known to issue press releases through an entity that has a name beginning with:

The Committee for . . .

The Alliance for . . .

The Association of . . .

Citizens for (or Against) . . .

Taxpayers for (or Against) . . .

The Coalition for . . .

Parents for . . .

The Foundation for . . .

The Institute of . . .

Is this tactic devious? Misleading? Unethical?

Sometimes. If the purpose of creating a "shadow" entity or group is to trick or mislead the media or the public, then it is wrong. If, on the other hand, creating a seemingly organized, focused entity to suggest acceptance, agreement, or support of your message is a course you choose, it is as legitimate a tactic as if the idea had come about independently.

Mothers Against Drunk Driving (MADD) evolved from the efforts of one angry woman who lost a child because of a drunk driver. She called friends who called friends, and an organization was born that became as important as its name suggests, but it began with one woman and an attention-getting name.

Citizens for Better Television began (and possibly ended) with a woman sending out press releases that complained about excessive sex and violence on television. The releases got attention and were used to develop media stories.

The National Rifle Association, the Rainbow Coalition, the National Right to Life Committee, and the Moral Majority are in the news frequently, and their spokespersons become familiar as they offer their comments on their various issues. Yet, few people among the larger general public know much about these organizations except their names, the assumption being that they are somehow influential and speaking for a particular constituency.

It is not always easy to come by information on these groups, which may consist of a single person, several people, a mailing list, or a group that actually meets on occasion. In any case, the media took them seriously and used their press releases:

Action for Corporate Accountability
American National Standards Institute
Center for Public Integrity
Christian Leaders for Responsible Television
Coalition Against Media/Marketing Prejudice
Coalition for a Smoke-free City
Committee to Defend Reproductive Rights
Council on Economic Priorities
Earth Island Action Group
Free Congress Foundation
Fundamentalists Anonymous
Interfaith Center on Corporate Responsibility
International Forum on Globalization
International Organization for Standardization
National Hispanic Media Coalition
National Institute of Justice
National Organization for Women
National Organization of Men
Natural Resources Defense Committee
Rain Forest Action Group
Rain Forest Action Network
U.S. Committee for Energy Awareness

Many of the names sound cause related, but the principle applies to products and companies as well. A statement from the Tobacco Institute, the Fur Institute, the Better Health Foundation, or the Automotive Institute may diffuse criticism and help sell cigarettes, furs, vitamins, and cars, respectively.

The Riverdale PTA will likely get its press release read by the editor of the *Riverdale News*. Other entities, less known, yet seeking publicity for a particular product, company, issue, or cause, may not find it quite so easy. The media as well as the public tend to prioritize and, until they are made to feel otherwise, will treat subjects with importance that *sound* important. Therefore, the press release for the Riverdale Book Club meeting will not likely get as much attention as one for the Greater Riverdale Citizens Literacy Council. That example may be an exaggeration, but not by much. To get attention, the subject must appear to be worthy of attention.

Don't lie or misrepresent what you are or what you have. However, you're fully within the rules to make what you have as interesting, fascinating, significant, and relevant as you can persuade any number of people to say it is. Much of publicity is "packaging," and if a more dignified-sounding entity issuing comments on your behalf presents your message in a nicer package, that's not bad.

A popular show-business performer was introduced on a TV variety show as "just possibly the most talented man in show business—a writer, musician, composer, actor, comedian . . . and genius." The performer came on stage, smiled, waved, and thanked the host for "that very kind, if somewhat embarrassing, introduction." The audience was never told that the performer had written his own introduction and handed it to the host to read.

Often the quickest way to become known as important or special is to tell people that you *are* important and special.

AT A GLANCE
GREAT EXPECTATIONS

- If you have prepared your plan well, the media that you contact will be receptive, rather than resistant or disinterested regarding your subject.

- It is the publicist's call that brings media attention to the material. You can't expect the material, no matter how dazzling, to do the job alone.

continued

- Successful media relationships are based on mutual trust. The media must know that the publicist will show respect for their time and deadlines, be honest, and act with integrity.

- Writing is a communication skill, and publicists should be able to write effectively on their subjects.

- Media deadlines are not flexible. Recognize this, and take and return reporters' calls promptly. Doing so can directly affect or influence how your subject will be treated by the media.

- Be professional in conversations with the media; choose your words carefully; be concise and well prepared.

- After each media contact, write a short summary for your files to keep a record of the conversation, noting any and all important facts related.

- Do not address subjects outside of your area of responsibility or expertise.

- Whenever possible, quote from and supply copies of authoritative written material.

- It is appropriate for a publicist to tell a reporter that certain requested information is confidential or proprietary and cannot be provided.

- Recognize that volunteers may need extra care and consideration in lieu of payment. Show appreciation.

- Have "brainstorming" sessions with volunteers. Good ideas can come from any number of places.

- Co-op publicity programs, like co-op advertising, put together more than one entity of common interests, to raise and reinforce the recognition of one another.

- For the added ring of authority, special interests have been known to recruit spokespersons and issue press releases through an entity with an authoritative, dignified, prestigious name.

6

Notes from the Field

FORMS AND SUBSTANCE: LOOKS AND WORKS

Press releases, newsletters, private showings are examples of publicists reaching out to tell a story, shape an image, beat the drum, and get noticed. How do they look? How do they work?

The following pages offer some examples of diverse interests trying to get the attention of a variety of constituencies: the general public, trade audiences, business-to-business, professional associates.

From a poet to the elite of the marketing profession; from a broker alliance to rock-and-roll stars; from an energy company to the public relations profession, these examples reveal a significant truth. That is that the *process* of generating attention and publicity is the same, whether it is directed at the trade press, a limited inner circle of friends, or the country at large.

All of these examples were produced by professionals on a variety of budgets and in a variety of quantities.

143

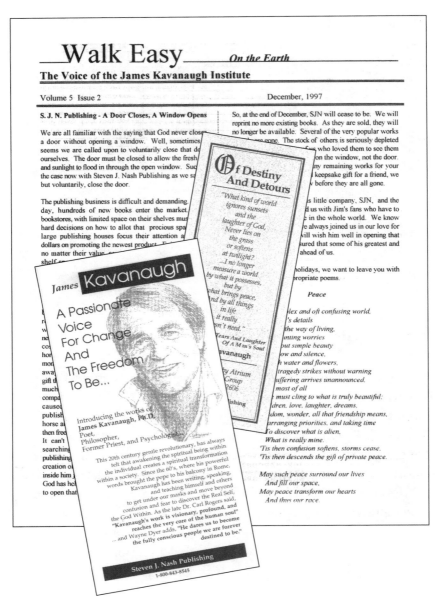

Walk Easy _____ *On the Earth*

The Voice of the James Kavanaugh Institute

Volume 5 Issue 2	December, 1997

S. J. N. Publishing - A Door Closes, A Window Opens

We are all familiar with the saying that God never closes a door without opening a window. Well, sometimes it seems we are called upon to voluntarily close that door ourselves. The door must be closed to allow the fresh and sunlight to flood in through the open window. Such the case now with Steven J. Nash Publishing as we but voluntarily, close the door.

The publishing business is difficult and demanding. day, hundreds of new books enter the market. bookstores, with limited space on their shelves mus hard decisions on how to allot that precious spa large publishing houses focus their attention a dollars on promoting the newest product. no matter their value shelf

So, at the end of December, SJN will cease to be. We will reprint no more existing books. As they are sold, they will no longer be available. Several of the very popular works gone. The stock of others is seriously depleted who loved them to see them on the window, not the door. my remaining works for your keepsake gift for a friend, we before they are all gone.

s little company, SJN, and the d us with Jim's fans who have to c in the whole world. We know e always joined us in our love for ill wish him well in opening that ured that some of his greatest and ahead of us.

holidays, we want to leave you with ropriate poems.

Peace

lex and oft confusing world.
's details
the way of living.
nting worries
but simple beauty
ow and silence.
h water and flowers.
tragedy strikes without warning
uffering arrives unannounced.
most of all
must cling to what is truly beautiful:
dren, love, laughter, dreams.
dom, wonder, all that friendship means.
arranging priorities, and taking time
To discover what is alien,
   What is really mine.
'Tis then confusion softens, storms cease.
'Tis then descends the gift of private peace.

May such peace surround our lives
   And fill our space,
May peace transform our hearts
   And thus our race.

Of Destiny And Detours

"What kind of world
ignores sunsets
and the
laughter of God,
Never lies on
the grass
or softens
at twilight?
...I no longer
measure a world
by what it possesses,
but by
what brings peace,
and by all things
in life
it really
isn't need."

*Tears And Laughter
Of A Man's Soul*

avanaugh

y Atrium
Group
2606
lishing

James Kavanaugh

A Passionate Voice For Change And The Freedom To Be...

Introducing the works of
James Kavanaugh, Ph.D.
Poet,
Philosopher,
Former Priest, and Psychologist

This 20th century gentle revolutionary, has always felt that awakening the spiritual being within the individual creates a spiritual transformation within a society. Since the 60's, where his powerful words brought the pope to his balcony in Rome, Kavanaugh has been writing, speaking, and teaching himself and others to get under our masks and move beyond confusion and fear to discover the Real Self, the God Within. As the late Dr. Carl Rogers said, "Kavanaugh's work is visionary, profound, and reaches the very core of the human soul" ... and Wayne Dyer adds, "He dares us to become the fully conscious people we are forever destined to be."

Steven J. Nash Publishing
1-800-843-8545

James Kavanaugh is one of America's bestselling poets, yet he keeps a relatively low profile. Through a controlled mailing list, Kavanaugh keeps in contact with his loyal audience, sending newsletters, tapes, brochures, catalogs, and news of upcoming appearances and forthcoming books.   Courtesy: Steven J. Nash Publishing

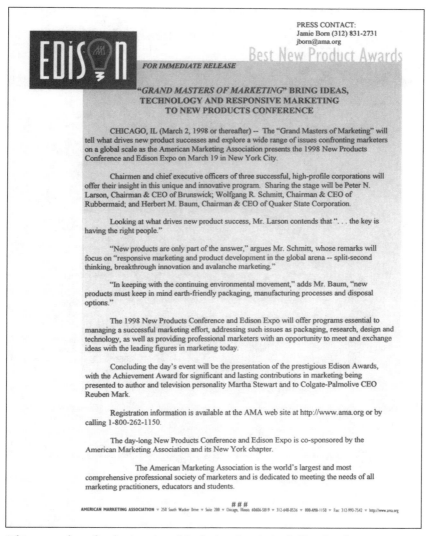

PRESS CONTACT:
Jamie Born (312) 831-2731
jborn@ama.org

Best New Product Awards

FOR IMMEDIATE RELEASE

**"GRAND MASTERS OF MARKETING" BRING IDEAS,
TECHNOLOGY AND RESPONSIVE MARKETING
TO NEW PRODUCTS CONFERENCE**

CHICAGO, IL (March 2, 1998 or thereafter) -- The "Grand Masters of Marketing" will tell what drives new product successes and explore a wide range of issues confronting marketers on a global scale as the American Marketing Association presents the 1998 New Products Conference and Edison Expo on March 19 in New York City.

Chairmen and chief executive officers of three successful, high-profile corporations will offer their insight in this unique and innovative program. Sharing the stage will be Peter N. Larson, Chairman & CEO of Brunswick; Wolfgang R. Schmitt, Chairman & CEO of Rubbermaid; and Herbert M. Baum, Chairman & CEO of Quaker State Corporation.

Looking at what drives new product success, Mr. Larson contends that ". . . the key is having the right people."

"New products are only part of the answer," argues Mr. Schmitt, whose remarks will focus on "responsive marketing and product development in the global arena -- split-second thinking, breakthrough innovation and avalanche marketing."

"In keeping with the continuing environmental movement," adds Mr. Baum, "new products must keep in mind earth-friendly packaging, manufacturing processes and disposal options."

The 1998 New Products Conference and Edison Expo will offer programs essential to managing a successful marketing effort, addressing such issues as packaging, research, design and technology, as well as providing professional marketers with an opportunity to meet and exchange ideas with the leading figures in marketing today.

Concluding the day's event will be the presentation of the prestigious Edison Awards, with the Achievement Award for significant and lasting contributions in marketing being presented to author and television personality Martha Stewart and to Colgate-Palmolive CEO Reuben Mark.

Registration information is available at the AMA web site at http://www.ama.org or by calling 1-800-262-1150.

The day-long New Products Conference and Edison Expo is co-sponsored by the American Marketing Association and its New York chapter.

The American Marketing Association is the world's largest and most comprehensive professional society of marketers and is dedicated to meeting the needs of all marketing practitioners, educators and students.

# # #

AMERICAN MARKETING ASSOCIATION ▼ 250 South Wacker Drive ▼ Suite 200 ▼ Chicago, Illinois 60606-5819 ▼ 312-648-0536 ▼ 800-AMA-1150 ▼ Fax: 312-993-7542 ▼ http://www.ama.org

This press release for the American Marketing Association's New Products Conference and Edison Expo uses "The Grand Masters of Marketing"—a panel of three of America's most marketing-savvy CEOs—to get the attention of the profession and build conference attendance. It worked. Courtesy: American Marketing Association

Author–TV personality Martha Stewart and Colgate CEO Reuben Mark each received the American Marketing Association's Edison Achievement Award and considerable media attention surrounding their appearance at the AMA's Edison Awards ceremony following a daylong conference of marketers. Courtesy: American Marketing Association

Brokers under fire at one of America's largest trading exchanges successfully told their side of the story in a series of newsletters that developed into a highly credible and respected industry publication.   Courtesy: National Alliance of Futures and Options Brokers, Traders and FCMs

BENDER
BROWNING
DOLBY &
SANDERSON

PUBLIC RELATIONS

Contact: Helen Kensick
        (312) 670-1139
           or
        Chris Garcia
        (312) 670-1131   EXCLUSIVE TO GEORGE LAZARUS

**HERE THEY COME, THE MONKEES, TO BENDER BROWNING
DOLBY & SANDERSON**

CHICAGO, ILLINOIS, June 17, 1996--Bender Browning Dolby & Sanderson Advertising, Inc.
announced today that they have been chosen as the public relations agency for the Monkees 30th
Anniversary tour. The Monkees reunion tour kicks off in mid June and spans coast to coast with
concerts in over 50 cities. Micky Dolenz, Peter Tork and Davy Jones are back and even better;
seasoned, more musically accomplished and full of the unexpected, hilarious antics that captured
America's heart via their breakthrough, Emmy award winning series.

     Outselling both the Beatles and the Rolling Stones combined in 1967, the Monkees charted
repeatedly with such classics as "I'm a Believer", "Last Train to Clarksville" and "Daydream
Believer". As television's first video band, the Monkees have become rock icons who appeal to an
unusually broad range of fans from the 60's and now their children who know the Monkees' series
as well as their music.

     The Monkees' manager, Ward Sylvester, also the original executive producer for the
Monkees, selected Bender Browning Dolby & Sanderson based on promotional work done by
Helen Kensick, Bender Browning's public relations manager, for Davy Jones when she was a
teenager. Her public relations career now spans 30 years. Jones, Sylvester, and Kensick met
while Jones was in the Broadway production of "Oliver!". Along came the Monkees and the rest
is history.

*Pop culture is alive and well as the Monkees, the legendary '60s made-for-TV rock-
and-roll band, reunite for a 30th Anniversary tour. The Chicago agency Bender
Browning Dolby & Sanderson is tapped to promote the event, and both the trade
and general-interest media take notice.*   Courtesy: Bender Browning Dolby & Sanderson
Advertising, Inc.

4 Star-Gazette, Thursday, August 1, 1996 **TIME OUT**

TOP HITS

TOP POP SINGLES
"Macarena (Bayside Boys mix)" Los Del Rio
"You're Makin' Me High/Let It Be," Toni Braxton
"California Love/How Do U Want It," 2Pac featuring Dr. Dre and Roger Troutman
"Give Me One Reason," Tracy Chapman
"I Can't Sleep Baby (If I)," R. Kelly
"Change the World," Eric Clapton
"Twisted," Keith Sweat
"You Learn," Alanis Morissette
"C'Mon N' Ride It (The Train)," Quad City DJ's
"Loungin'," L.L. Cool J

TOP-SELLING ALBUMS
"It Was Written," NAS
"Jagged Little Pill," Alanis Morissette
"Blue," Leann Rimes
"Load," Metallica
"E. 1999 Eternal," Bone Thugs-N-Harmony
"Secrets," Toni Braxton
"The Score," Fugees
"Falling Into You," Celine Dion
"New Beginning," Tracy Chapman

Music

Hey hey, they're back!

Monkees regroup in 30th anniversary tour, album project

By DANIEL ALOI
Star-Gazette

They were originally brought together for a TV series and called "The Pre-Fab Four," but The Monkees did master their music.

They topped the charts and broke new ground even after new episodes of the series ceased in the late '60s – until Peter Tork and then Michael Dolenz and Davy Jones continued while Dolenz

Monkees (Davy Jones, Peter Tork) reshaped in 1986 for their 20th ... released an album with Mike Nesmith.

IN CONCERT

■ The Monkees' 30th Anniversary Tour will make two stops in the area:
■ Monday at the Anderson Center, Binghamton University. Tickets are $29.50 reserved, $15 lawn, at the box office (1-888-BINGFEST toll-free) or Ticketmaster.
■ Thursday, Aug. 22 at Finger Lakes Performing Arts Center in Canandaigua. Tickets are $25.50 reserved; $12.50 lawn. To order, call 716/222-5000 or 800/722-3938.

---

14 Wednesday, October 30, 1996   THE EVANSVILLE PRESS

Trio of Monkees will perform here Friday

ENTERTAINMENT

Fans still screaming three decades later

By Sandra Knipe
Entertainment reporter

Thirty years ago, Peter Tork probably would have laughed at the idea that at 54, he'd still be a Monkee, performing for thousands of screaming fans.

On the suggestion that he scared him to death.

"The truth is I did not understand if nearly as well as I am. I was very confused for as a kid. I didn't get it," said Tork, one of a trio of Monkees, including Micky Dolenz and Davy Jones, who will perform here Friday as part of the group's 30th anniversary tour.

The concert sponsored by Casino Aztar will be Michael Nesmith, who will perform at a few select venues.

Over time, Tork, who used to be considered the "dumb" one Monkee, come to realize that "what was going on was that we were [their] projections.

"We were the screen on which the children of Middle America were projecting their frustrations. A kid comes out of that off that ...

Do you ...

Hey, hey, it's ...
once a ...

Courtesy photo

... Peter Tork and Davy Jones.

NEW CAMPAIGNS

The Monkees come to Bender Browning Dolby & Sanderson

(left to right): Micky Dolenz, Peter Tork and Davy Jones.

Bender Browning Dolby & Sanderson Advertising, Inc. was chosen as the public relations agency for the Monkees 30th Anniversary tour, which spans coast to coast with concerts in over 50 cities.

Outselling both the Beatles and the Rolling Stones combined in 1967, the Monkees charted repeatedly with such classics as "I'm a Believer," "Last Train to Clarksville" and "Daydream Believer." As television's first video band, the Monkees have become rock icons who appeal to a broad range of fans from the 60's and now their children who know their series as well as their music.

The Monkees' manager, Ward Sylvester, also its original executive producer, selected Bender Browning Dolby & Sanderson based on promotional work done by Helen Kensick, Bender Browning's public relations manager.

Other 30th Anniversary celebrations include Rhino Records' marketing campaign with Musicland, the official retailer of the Monkees' tour, which include freestanding in-store displays showcasing the extensive Rhino Monkees audio and video catalog.

A 75-minute documentary of the band is currently in the works with the Disney Channel.

Bender Browning also represented the Monkees in 1989 for their successful legal battle with Columbia Pictures over the right to use their name and logo.

..., Peter Tork and Davy Jones.

Now, in addition to touring and recording with the Monkees and occasional guest spots on television shows, he performs acoustic folk-rock with singing partner James Lee Stanley.

Besides "Justus," a recently released Monkees album which includes Nesmith, Tork has his own new album, "Stranger Things Have Happened," which features Nesmith and Dolenz on "Milkshake," a tune about the nightmare of life on the road.

Tork doesn't seem to consider it such a nightmare anymore.

"I don't males are 50 or 20 ... screaming females are ... pondering about what it means ... be part of watching 20-year-... screaming over these for-... teen-age heart throbs. Not ... we know just 20-year-old ... over — but we're not Dad. ... and we're not dead either."

The Monkees will perform at 8:30 p.m. Friday at Van Auditorium. Tickets ... for the general public ... Casino Aztar premier Club members ... information, call 433-... 800) DIAL-FUN.

444 NORTH MICHIGAN AVENUE
SUITE 1400
CHICAGO, ILLINOIS 60611
312/644.9600

BBDM PUBLIC RELATIONS

Contact: Helen Kensick   FOR IMMEDIATE RELEASE
             or
          Maureen Kite
          (312) 644-9600

                    DAVY JONES RELEASES AUTOBIOGRAPHY,

                    THEY MADE A MONKEE OUT OF ME

        CHICAGO, IL, FEBRUARY   -- With pop history coming full

circle as Monkeemania once again sweeps the country, Davy Jones

comically portrays his life as a Monkee, jockey, actor and Broadway

performer in his new autobiography, They Made a Monkee Out of Me.

        He will be at Flash Entertainment, 30th & K Streets, Sacramento,

on Sunday, March 6, at 1:00 p.m., to autograph copies of his new book.

        Full of unexpected antics, candid glimpses into an unprecedented

show business phenomenon, and hilarious, episodic anecdotes, Jones'

autobiography is also a visual chronicle containing 400 photographs.

        "As tv's first video band, the Monkees created a whole new form

of entertainment. We're back and we're better- - - -seasoned, more

musically accomplished and we have a new working atmosphere on stage,"

says Jones regarding the recent revival of the Monkees who recently

completed a national concert tour.

        Their recent album "Pool It" has just sold gold and a Monkees movie

is underway.

Pop singer–actor Davy Jones launches a publicity campaign to promote his autobiography, They Made a Monkee Out of Me, *recalling his ups and downs with the made-for-TV rock band, the Monkees.*   Courtesy: Bender Browning Dolby & Sanderson

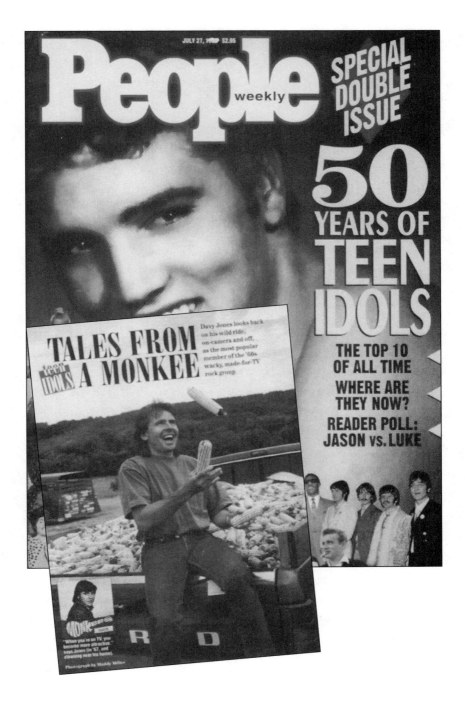

Amoco Laser Company
1809 Mill Street
Naperville, Illinois 60540
312-369-4190

Contact: Helen Kensick   FOR IMMEDIATE RELEASE
          (312) 644-9600

                 AMOCO LASER COMPANY INTRODUCES

                 MINIATURIZED, MORE POWERFUL LASERS

     BALTIMORE, MD, April 27   -- Amoco Laser Company, a wholly
owned subsidiary of Amoco Corporation, today announced the introduction
of a family of miniaturized laser products developed from its
revolutionary microlaser technology.

     "Vastly smaller, more efficient, and superior in performance,
microlasers can be mass produced at significantly reduced costs,"
according to Tom Wolfram, general manager of Amoco Laser Company.
"A technological breakthrough, microlasers will not only replace
existing gas tube discharge lasers, but will also stimulate new product
development in consumer markets."

     "Capable of improving the quality of high resolution projection
television, film scanners and color printers, microlasers will also
facilitate new radar scanners for aircraft and automobile collision
avoidance systems," Wolfram adds.

     Amoco's microlasers represent the first uniform technology that
can address virtually all laser applications requiring green, blue,

*Amoco, one of the best-known oil companies in the world, needed to establish its
expertise and its credibility in the field of laser technology. This is one of several press
releases in a press kit that helped to tell its story.*   Courtesy: Amoco and Bender Browning
Dolby & Sanderson Advertising, Inc.

Thomas L. Harris, a founder of the giant public relations firm Golin/Harris Communications, publishes a quarterly newsletter that offers analysis and commentary on industry events, while keeping Mr. Harris's profile high among leading spokespersons for his profession. Courtesy: Thomas L. Harris & Associates

FIELD NOTES

Publicists, check your calendars!

Virtually every newspaper has a "Calendar of Upcoming Events" section. It is the backbone of weekly newspapers and is typically found on Fridays and/or Sundays in the big (and often not-so-big) daily papers. To the public it's a calendar, but to publicists it is a list of upcoming publicity projects.

From poetry readings to the auto show preview to a demonstration of gymnastics skills to a seminar on keeping a journal or dealing with loneliness, inclusion in the newspaper calendar section is formula stuff to most publicists. Often there is no charge for listing, but just as often the wall between the advertising department and the news department finds itself with a few holes in it. As with the telephone directory, a generic listing may be free, but to be listed in boldface type or to add a slogan, a description of what you do, the founder's name, or a few lines of simple text can all be worked out for a fee.

Publicists looking for potential publicity ideas should take note of the calendar section not only for posting appropriate items and events but also for ideas that might well be adapted or may inspire other ideas or events. For example, in Chicago, Marshall Field's department store often runs a two-column (or wider) vertical ad under its logo and the heading "Field Notes." Although these listings are a part of the store's ad, they are the store's own "calendar of events," noting upcoming store activities over a period of days or weeks. The activities are basically all publicity events, such as these which are drawn from three separate "Field Notes" over a period of four months:

- **The Clock Strikes 100**
A celebration of the 100th anniversary of the store's famous clock. Visit the store's clock shop between November 16 and November 26 and view the original Norman Rockwell painting of the clock, featured on a *Saturday Evening Post* cover in 1945.

- **Shirley Corriher Signing**

Meet the international speaker, food writer, and "culinary food sleuth," who will autograph copies of her book *Cookwise: The Hows & Whys of Successful Cooking with 250 Great-Tasting Recipes.*

- **Meet Arthur During Baby Days**

Over a four-day period, the world's most famous aardvark, immortalized in children's books as well as a hit PBS-TV series, will appear at three of the store's locations, in the Kids' Department, where Arthur's new baby sister Baby Kate, an adorable plush, will be introduced.

- **Meet Designer Susan Horton**

The fashion designer will appear in the Men's Department at two store locations over a two-day period to demonstrate her knitwear technique and present her scarf collection.

- *Vogue* **Holiday Fashion Show**

- **Dress Your Home for the Holidays**

Learn exciting ways to entertain as Field's shares its ideas on creating a wonderful table setting, whether it be formal or casual. Following the presentation, a representative from Christopher Radko will present holiday decorating tips.

- **ZooLights Festival**

The store sponsors Chicago's Lincoln Park's annual presentation of more than 50 animated and whimsical light displays, featuring spectacular ice-carvings, musical entertainment, children's craft activities, visits with Santa, and animal viewing.

- **The Great Tree**

A beloved tradition at the store, based on the holiday classic *Nutcracker.* The Great Tree, the annual holiday windows, and the store's main aisles are decorated with illustrations from author Maurice Sendak's version of *Nutcracker.* The theme extends to ornaments designed as the Nutcracker, the Mouse King, toy drums, and heart-shaped cookies.

- **Helen Boehm Signing**

At this exclusive event, Mrs. Boehm will sign purchases of Boehm, including "The Christmas Rose" sculpture in the store's Collectors Gallery.

- **Hermes Scarf-Tying Event**

Join Hermes representative Rachel Fagin for "Tying the Knot—The Fine Art of Hermes Scarf Tying" and view the fall/winter collection of Hermes accessories for men and women at the store's Hermes Boutique.

- **Nambe Annual Signing with Karim Rashid**

Designer Karim Rashid will make an exclusive appearance at four stores over a three-day period, to sign Nambe Studio purchases of his design Silver.

- **The Beauty of Christmas**

Several cast members of Disney's *Beauty and the Beast,* currently appearing on stage, will be performing carols from their compact disc *The Beauty of Christmas,* with proceeds from the sale of the disc going to benefit Broadway Cares/Equity Fights AIDS.

- **Meet Amy Coleman**

KitchenAid presents the host of the PBS-TV show *Cooking with Amy Coleman,* sharing some of her holiday recipes. During the event, copies of the book *Home Cooking with Amy Coleman* will be offered as a free gift with any KitchenAid purchase of $75 or more.

- **Kosta Boda and Orrefors Personalizing Event**

At four stores over a three-day period, the store will engrave a special message with the purchase of Kosta Boda and Orrefors crystal during this special personalizing event, in the store's Crystal Gallery.

- **Meet Sarah Kirwan Blazek**

The author will read and autograph her book *An Irish Night Before Christmas,* in the Book Department.

- **Prom 1998**

Model Cindi Hodgkins demonstrates a glamorous look from head to toe with key tips for the prom—on gown selection, make-up, hair, and accessories, at four store locations over two consecutive weekends.

- **Belleek Signing**

Artisan Karina Bogle will sign purchases of Belleek Parian china, including a vase exclusive to this event, at a showing of a special collection of designer pieces, starting at $1,000, in the China Department of three stores over a three-day period.

- *Forever Plaid* **Performance**

A special performance during a Friday afternoon lunch hour by cast members of the long-running musical hit *Forever Plaid,* part of the store's TreatSeats program, which invites guests to register and win tickets to a performance or take advantage of TreatSeats discount coupons.

- **Peter Rabbit Hosts an Easter Egg Hunt**

In a celebration of "Beatrix Potter—A Storybrook Spring," Peter Rabbit visits two stores over Easter weekend to meet the children, pose for photographs, and lead a search for eggs filled with tasty treats.

- **Men's Shopping Night**

On a "special (Thursday) night of shopping" in the Men's Bridge Department, gentlemen are invited to enjoy a martini, light refreshments, and informal modeling, as designer representatives from DKNY, Mondo di Marco, Wilke Rodriguez, Jhane Barnes, Ted Baker, and Gene Meyer stand by to assist with their selections.

- **Calvin Klein Men's Spring Preview**

Calvin Klein's Spring Men's Collection will be informally modeled, with designer representatives on hand to assist shoppers with their selections.

- **Liz Petites Wardrobing Seminar**

A Liz Petites wardrobing seminar with a New York representative demonstrating how to create the perfect look from head to toe. A $5 ticket purchase is required with all proceeds going to benefit the United Way, with refreshments served.

- **Urban Gateways Performing Artists**

Every day during lunch hours over two weeks in the Atrium of the downtown store, guests are invited to enjoy musical and dance performances from around the world by artists from Urban Gateways—The Center for Arts in Education.

Authors appearing at a book-signing event are not unusual, even if the author is relatively unknown, so why not designers, sculptors, and anyone else who would put their names on their creations? The possibilities are limitless.

LOOKING IN THE WINDOW

The same Marshall Field's department store noted with its calendar of events has been credited with maintaining a holiday tradition for years: each Christmas season, Field's downtown flagship store decorates its windows with holiday scenes, usually following a theme, which have included *Toyland, The Night Before Christmas,* and *The Silver Skates.*

Other large department stores around the United States create similar storybook windows or Christmas scenes, often incorporating elaborate productions. Lord & Taylor in New York, for example, presented Charles Dickens's *A Christmas Carol* in its Fifth Avenue store windows. The unveiling ceremony featured Hal Linden, star of television and Broadway, who was appearing in a New York stage production of the Dickens classic. The program also featured the P.S. 95–Eastwood International Children's Choir and Carolers.

The store also announced that "In the true spirit of the season, Lord & Taylor and American Express will make a donation to City Harvest, the nation's oldest and largest food rescue program. Each time you make a purchase at Lord & Taylor with your American Express card . . . you will be helping to feed more than 60,000 people a week in New York City."

The celebration would continue for weeks, with appearances by Jeane-Marie Dickens, founder of the Charles Dickens Heritage Foundation; a display of Dickens's original manuscript of *A Christmas Carol* at the Morgan Library; and a drawing to win an all-expense-paid trip for two to "Victorian England," theater tickets, gift certificates, dinners, and collectible *Scrooge* figurines.

Viewing store windows as a family is suggested as a holiday activity. Turning the event into something both warm and historical that, at the same time, benefits needy families positions the store as above mere merchandising, wins goodwill, spreads good cheer, and, not incidentally, draws people who might otherwise not have come to look at the store.

IN THE CARDS

To paraphrase the overused ad line, "This is not your father's credit card." Credit cards used to be for making purchases easier and more convenient, but that's all changed. Not only is there a seemingly endless choice of credit cards and bank charge cards, but for publicists, it also can certainly be worth a press release (with photo), a launch party, and perhaps a contest or two, to present credit cards bearing the likeness of Elvis, a favorite hometown team, zoo animals, antique cars, historical figures, Batman . . .

Ford and General Motors cards are part of a purchase promotion. Each purchase using the card accrues points which may be applied to rebates on purchases of the companies' respective automobiles. As joint promotions go, the underwriting banks want to put the cards in customers' hands, and the automakers want to sell cars, not to be in the financing business, so both sides get what they want. Benefits are to the customer, and the publicist gets to give the papers an "everybody wins" story.

AND THE AWARD GOES TO . . .

Much of the general public remembers when it was the Oscars and the Emmys, with maybe the Grammys or Tonys, but that was pretty much it. Then TV producers and publicists got together and saw the value of an award to help sell a movie, a TV series or special, or a record album, or to just generally boost about a dozen or so careers, while feeding the public's hunger for celebrities. So, enter the People's Choice Awards, the Golden Globe Awards, the Country Music Awards, the American Music Awards, the American Film Institute Awards, the Kennedy Center Honors, and the list goes on.

Time magazine has its "Man of the Year."

The advertising industry presents Addies, Cleos, and Eagles.

The American Marketing Association has the Edison Awards for Achievement, Marketer of the Year, and Best New Product of the Year.

Disney presents the Golden Apple Awards to distinguished schoolteachers.

There's the National Book Award, the Pulitzer Prize, and the Nobel Prize.

Nearly every town, every industry, every profession or trade association has its person, place, or thing of the year. If publicists had their way, there would be more of them.

And, just when one might suspect there would not be time for one more, comes the *Time for Peace Awards,* sponsored by Concord watchmakers. The award is for "An ever evolving challenge to the creative spirit in all of us. The harmony of many sounds . . . the unity of many images . . . the brilliance of vision balanced by tolerance and understanding. From inspiration to realization, peace is concept, craft and commitment . . . in perfect concord."

And, as publicists have learned, there's always room on the wall for another award.

WHEN THE INTERVIEW IS CONFIRMED

This actually happens. After much back-and-forth over scheduling, it's confirmed. The publicist's boss or client will tape the interview at the television studio for a segment to be included in the evening news report.

The most likely questions to be asked are rehearsed, and everyone's comfortable. The boss/client gets a haircut. And a new jacket. And calls the in-laws to remind them to watch the evening news. The taping goes beautifully.

The people gather around their respective television sets and watch the evening news—including commercials—from beginning to end. The interview does not appear. There was no phone call to say the segment had been bumped and no apparent big breaking story that would have understandably preempted the piece. It just simply didn't run. The boss/client is embarrassed and trying not to appear angry, as that might be viewed as a sign of an inflated ego. The publicist is at a loss to explain what happened or, more correctly, didn't happen.

A call the next morning to the producer receives the response, "We were running long. These things happen all the time. Maybe we can do something at another time."

Well, these things *don't* happen all the time, but they *do* happen often enough that they are not unusual. It may seem inconsiderate, insensitive, and a very unprofessional waste of everyone's time, but it happens. Like the scenes from the film that end up on the cutting-room floor or the terrific number that was axed from the show, interviews can be canceled at the last minute, and interviews that make it to tape and editing may never run. To try to find an explanation that makes sense is pretty much an additional waste of time.

The publicist has to stand there while the boss/client says that he or she doesn't have time to waste on this sort of thing. The publicist also cannot afford to pass along any such dressing-down to the TV producer because that could well close the door to the possibility of doing something in the future.

Situations such as this underscore the need for the publicist to keep expectations realistic. Each day reporters tape conversations and call sources for comments that never appear in the final stories. The publicist must keep reminding the boss/client that sometimes things happen that can cause a segment to be shortened considerably or not run at all. In the words of Mel Brooks, "Hope for the best; expect the worst."

A possible way of salvaging the experience—turning a setback into an opportunity—is to create a press release based on the material covered in the TV interview. Presumably the boss/client got off a good quote or two in the interview, and such comments could form the basis of a policy statement on a timely subject. Don't be surprised if after the story runs in the morning paper, you receive a call about doing something on that very subject for the evening TV news.

7

A Crash Course in Publicity

In real estate it is said that the three most important considerations are *location, location,* and *location.* For a successful publicity program, it might be said that the three things are *planning, planning, planning.*

Obviously the execution part of the plan is no minor consideration, but with reputations, integrity, and a subject's public image on the line, publicists are best advised to plan well how a publicity effort will be structured, what elements will go into it, and what alternatives are possible if the plan needs modification or radical surgery.

Essentially a publicity effort involves: The Plan.

Whatever the subject (a company, product, service organization, practice, trade association, partnership, cause, candidate, group—whether profit or nonprofit),

- Set an objective—what you want to do.
- Identify the people involved—managers, founders, principals, spokespersons, talent.
- Collect the information—a media kit with the essential information you will need to tell your story.
- Define your strategy—the approach you will take to reach your objectives.
- Create a list of tactics—create and disseminate press releases, photographs, posters; hold press conferences,

events, tours, media appearances, and interviews; develop a program of mailings, signage, and phone follow-ups.

Clearly, as each publicist's plan will have distinct differences, some of the following suggestions may have greater or lesser importance than others, or will be listed in a different order. But, as crash courses go, these 101 specific points aimed at generating good publicity will help the publicist to create an outline, a structure, checklist, map, or (ahem) a *plan* that will make some of the elements of the publicity process more efficient and less mysterious.

101 Points to Help You Create a Publicity Program

1. Set goals and objectives. In writing.

People have a tendency to remember things differently. Planning is essential to a good publicity program, and clearly defined objectives are essential to good planning. It is not helpful, however, when people are not clear about what they agreed to do. Putting objectives in writing not only helps keep all participants in the effort moving toward the same goal, but also offers psychological value. People are conditioned to believe something that is in writing—even if they've written it themselves.

2. Identify your target audience(s).

It is entirely possible to aim at a target big enough to miss. The Lifetime cable TV network's slogan is "television for women," and it may very well offer something for every woman's taste at some point during a day, week, month, or season. But a typical publicity effort, to be successful, should define its audience as narrowly as possible. If the audience is women: Are they younger? Older? Affluent? Working mothers? College educated? Politically aware? The narrower the target audience, the less preconditioning of the environment may be necessary. The broader the audience, the greater the effort needed to bring everyone to the point where the message will strike a responsive chord. Define your audience in the most specific terms possible.

3. KNOW ALL THAT YOU CAN ABOUT WHAT PEOPLE THINK OF YOUR SUBJECT.

It is not unusual to hear someone say, "I know my customers" or "I know my market" or "I know my competition very well" . . . and then watch their effort fail because they were operating on assumptions: what they *thought* they knew, not what they *actually* knew. Market research, surveys, polling, and focus groups will help you better understand your target audience's likes and dislikes, or willingness to spend money or support a cause or an issue, but, much more important, market research can help you learn what your constituents think of you, your company, your product or service, your profession and industry, issues, causes, and concerns. A publicist representing a financial client is bound by certain restrictions (the things the Securities and Exchange Commission says a company can't say about itself to potential investors). Remember, however, that representatives of the securities industry, like any other particular group, may well have a predisposition one way or another about your subject.

An important part of publicizing a subject with the intention of influencing people's feelings about that subject is knowing somewhat how people feel in general.

4. IDENTIFY OR CREATE A USP—A UNIQUE SELLING POINT.

Whatever the subject of your publicity effort, it must be worthy of people's attention before it will receive that attention. The unique selling point is the element that makes what you have different from that of competitors or rivals, and worth knowing. Can a subject be publicized that is not at all unique? Yes, but to support, embrace, or patronize a product, company, or cause, the public typically requires not only that there be a defined value but also that the subject have a worthiness beyond what is average.

5. IDENTIFY BENEFITS FOR YOUR AUDIENCE RELATING TO YOUR SUBJECT.

People buy, vote, support, or advocate based on what the subject means to them. Sometimes it is brighter hair, whiter teeth, more value for the money, a better guarantee, or something as simple as philosophical agreement with a company or an issue. Some people won't buy Domino's pizza because the company's founder is a very public advocate of the "Right to Life" antiabortion issue; others will buy *only* Domino's pizza for the very same reason. How the pizza tastes or what it costs is a secondary concern to these people. Publicity has influenced how they feel and how they will react to the company and its products. A company that is "environmentally friendly" or "politically correct" or liberal or conservative may engender every bit as much brand loyalty as the company that offers quality, service, value, style, and a money-back guarantee. Whatever the subject, the audience wants to know what's in it for them. Tell them.

6. IDENTIFY YOUR COMPETITORS.

Some subject entities recognize the value to themselves strategically in both knowing all they can about their rivals, competitors, and opponents, and *defining* their competitors in public comparisons, taste tests, lab tests, and customer-satisfaction surveys. It is a risky strategy to identify competitors by name and "take them on" rather than just focusing on your subject exclusively, but such aggressiveness has often been rewarded with the products', companies', or candidates' achieving leadership status because they claimed it.

7. CREATE A BUDGET TO SUPPORT YOUR PLAN.

Publicity campaigns can be every bit as effective as advertising at a small fraction of the cost if handled correctly, but that does not mean there aren't *any* costs. Some people or brands that have received a tremendous amount of "free" publicity have incurred significant costs and expenses along the way. When setting objectives, determining strategies, and creating a plan, include a realistic budget for publicists' fees, travel, printing, promotions, events, direct mail, press conferences, media tours, and related costs. Something as seemingly simple as a CEO flying to Washington to be photographed attending an awards dinner can represent several thousand dollars of this year's budget. Understand it and plan accordingly to realistically fund publicity efforts.

8. ADAPT AND USE APPROPRIATE EXISTING MATERIALS.

What people managing large publicity efforts have in common with people running small publicity efforts is that neither of them want to spend any more money than is absolutely necessary. Most of the larger operations have to negotiate, fight, or beg for a budget to do the job, while the smaller programs not only don't *have* the money, but also usually don't even have anyone to ask for it. One obstacle to overcome is the prejudice against using something that is not new or fresh or, worst of all, might have been created by the current publicist's predecessor. To put it simply, if the funding's not there, the ego shouldn't be there either. Make the best of what you've got.

The press kit is the essential tool of the publicity campaign, containing press releases, backgrounders, fact sheets, photographs, annual reports, and reprints of particularly good articles that have recently appeared in trade journals or newsletters. It is surprisingly common for a publicist to ask a company or client for a sample press kit and to be told none exists. Too often then the publicist will begin creating the press kit from scratch, ignoring any materials that might exist on the grounds that they were "before my time." Ego aside, a good case can be made for the publicist's assembling as much material as possible and, from it, constructing a press kit that would be sufficient for at least the short term and reflect a certain consistency or continuity with the subject's past, as well as save money. Current updated photos and backgrounders are always a good idea, as these items need to be regularly freshened-up anyway, but a smart-looking folder, brochures, reprints, and the annual report don't need to be redone just for vanity's sake. Even pieces from an old ad campaign could serve as historical notations and be entertaining inclusions.

9. EVALUATE MATERIALS FOR FLEXIBILITY AS WELL AS EFFECTIVENESS.

As noted, photographs, backgrounders, and fact sheets should be updated regularly both to reflect the most current information and to keep the press kit looking fresh. Only the most recent press releases should be included in the press kit. Numbers change, events take place; a sense of timeliness reflected in the material suggests efficiency. Don't allow the colorful printed brochures or reports to be all you have to say. Typewritten inclusions to media materials convey a sense of immediacy, or at least current events, and are very cost effective to revise and update on a regular basis.

10. DESIGNATE A SINGLE SPOKESPERSON AS THE MEDIA CONTACT.

The publicist should be the designated spokesperson for the subject. The CEO can be quoted in press releases, bylined articles, or speech reprints and offered for interviews, but the CEO should not be the day-to-day spokesperson for the subject. Theoretically, the CEO has more and better things to do, and to be the apparently full-time media contact diminishes the importance of the officer's role and position. Further, the publicist should be responsible for getting quotes and comments from the appropriate source within the company or organization. This function should not fall to the CEO, nor to a "fill-in" coordinator recruited from the secretarial pool. A single spokesperson as contact makes it easier for the media, should be a more streamlined arrangement for the company or client, and keeps ill-informed, less-informed, or unauthorized persons from speaking to the media about matters that may be outside their fields of experience.

11. COORDINATE THE PUBLICITY EFFORT WITH THE AD PROGRAM AND/OR MARKETING CAMPAIGN.

On occasion, when publicity, advertising, marketing, shareholder relations, and/or corporate PR are handled by different agencies or by different individuals within an organization (and perhaps guided by separate budgets), "turf wars" may occur. The worst extreme is that the subject entity appears to be disorganized and inefficient and speaks to its constituency with more than one voice. The appearance of efficiency, consistency, and good organization is essential to a successful publicity program. Designate a single individual to see that the publicity program, ad campaign, and any other public- or marketing-related program all reflect the central focus of the subject's message and appear to be unified and consistent.

12. BE CLEAR ABOUT EXPECTATIONS ATTACHED TO THE PUBLICITY EFFORT.

Just as setting objectives is important, realistic assumptions about what can be achieved, at what expense, and through whose efforts are important as well. The cover of *Business Week,* an in-depth analysis in the *Wall Street Journal,* becoming a household word, and a million dollars' worth of "free" publicity are some common fantasies of those who would commission a publicity program. Those who would, alas, be charged with making the plan come to life might have a differing view of the subject and what is attainable. Perhaps the publicist was thinking more along the lines of a slow, consistent broadening of the subject's presence and influence in the trade press, a series of feature pieces, and executive interviews in newsletters and trade journals. Both reflect an objective of becoming more visible or prominent within a particular industry.

Sometimes publicity efforts are deemed to be less than successful because participants haven't acknowledged that they simply saw things differently and never quite agreed on what they expected the program to accomplish. A written statement of objectives, signed by all participants in the publicity effort, goes a long way to alleviating problems or misunderstandings. The adage goes, "I will almost certainly fail to meet your expectations if I don't know what your expectations are." Agree on what to expect.

13. BE CLEAR ABOUT WHO WILL BE RESPONSIBLE FOR WHAT AND TO WHOM.

Just as confusion can arise over expectations not met, a very common problem is characterized by the phrase ". . . but I thought *you* were going to take care of that!" especially in situations where the publicity committee, publicity chairperson, event chairperson, board of directors, marketing director, PR manager, or (fill in the blank) are all involved to some degree and each wants to play some role in the process.

This is another instance in which the written word can save time, confusion, swearing, and furniture throwing. Most publicity programs are tied to a specified time frame, and eliminating any confusion over who will be responsible for what facets of the plan, and during what period or phase, will save headaches and avoid duplicating efforts, but more important, it will increase the likelihood of the tasks' being done.

The question of who's in charge must also be dealt with. Whether the chairperson of a committee of volunteers outranks the salaried director of PR is a question to which there is no textbook answer. It will truly vary among companies and organizations. Line responsibility for decisions and reporting relationships are as important as who has the authority to sign purchase orders and checks. Be clear about your chain of command.

14. DETERMINE PROCEDURES FOR KEEPING ALL NECESSARY PARTICIPANTS IN THE PUBLICITY EFFORT INFORMED—AND FOR BEING KEPT INFORMED.

Few occurrences can be as upsetting to an executive, a board member, or even a staff person as having to learn fifth-hand of something the person feels he or she should have been made aware of. This happens often in publicity programs, where appearances, interviews, broadcasts, articles, and other printed comments can occur quickly or be moved up or back on the calendar.

The simplest solution—although it involves generating yet another document—is for the publicist to simply circulate a weekly (or as often as needed) memo or report noting the week's upcoming events and any changes in the schedule or plan. The reverse side of the problem—keeping the publicist informed of changes—is a bit more complicated. More than a few excellent publicists have walked out of a project after having assured a reporter that the status of a subject was one way, only to have a rival reporter learn from an inside source that something quite different was afoot.

It is not unusual in any large company, service group, practice, institution, campaign, or association for communication to occasionally break down and for an item to fall between the cracks. When the crack that's missed is represented by the publicist, who is the frontline contact with the media and the world, the issue takes on greater weight and embarrassment. For this reason, the publicist must create a "hot list" of phone numbers and do the equivalent of a morning bed check. It can be as simple as a quick call to the CEO's secretary or assistant or a voice-mail message left to remind the publicist of any breaking information that may affect the success of the publicity program. E-mail, voice mail, and interoffice communication vehicles are only as good as people's willingness to remember to use them.

15. CREATE OR AGREE ON A MECHANISM FOR RESPONDING TO INQUIRIES AND DETERMINING WHO WILL RESPOND.

Posting a contact's phone number on a press release; creating a "hot line" for communicating questions, problems, or information; and sending a postage-paid envelope to facilitate communication are standard procedures, but what distinguishes the professional publicist who succeeds from the mere functionaries is the speed, form, and effectiveness of the response to such inquiries.

The legend goes that somewhere a publicist loses his or her wings every time the phrase "was unavailable for comment" or "did not return phone calls" appears in a media account of an event. The publicist's role is to be responsive to inquiries in a way that respects both media deadlines and the importance of the subject. Timeliness is critical, but being able to deliver either information or a satisfactory statement of how long it will be until the information is available can determine both the amount and the quality of coverage a subject receives as well as the degree to which the publicist might influence the story on behalf of his or her cause.

With E-mail, voice mail, pagers, beepers, and cellular phones, there are fewer reasons why a response can't be handled quickly and efficiently. As with a press release, it is appropriate to have one person as the designated media contact, regardless of the subject. The contact can then bring in or collect information from another person, if necessary. In the age of information overload, it is wise to follow up phone conversations with a brief E-mail message, fax, or other form of documentation of the information communicated.

16. DETERMINE A CONTINGENCY OR EMERGENCY PLAN AND BUDGET FOR DEALING WITH A "WORST-CASE" SCENARIO.

This one is the black bag, the red phone, and the glass you break in case of emergencies. It's the plan you hope you will never have to implement but better have at the ready: your crisis plan.

Airlines stay in business by not crashing airplanes, but by the nature of what they do, the people in charge of airlines know the realities of their business and allow for the possibility of a crash. Unlike a highway accident, an airline disaster, almost by definition, means major losses . . . and major publicity. Similarly every business, practice, and industry must allow for the possibility of a crisis worthy of publicity and be prepared with a response plan. Consider your subject and what the *worst possible public disaster* might be. Exxon had the *Valdez* oil spill; Tylenol had reported deaths traced to product tampering; America Online "went dark" for 20 hours in 1996, and none of its millions of customers could get access to the nation's largest on-line service provider. The Democratic party was charged with accepting illegal political campaign contributions.

Each incident was front-page news. The media wanted the latest details and comments on the current situations and, while they were at it, some info on the management, history, successes, and failures over the years.

The subject entity should gear at least a part of its publicity effort to building goodwill with its public and industry. This goodwill may have to be exploited at such a time that a crisis occurs. The publicist also does not want the first information that people receive about the subject to be *bad* news. Consider what, if any, crises have occurred in your subject industry. Look at how the people or companies involved handled the situation, and learn from it. Develop your own list of potential crises, and have a response plan ready in reserve. It is simply a matter of being prepared.

On a noncrisis level, review your publicity plan to make certain it has enough flexibility to allow for adjustments, should conditions change along the way.

17. MAKE CERTAIN THAT ANY AND ALL LEGAL CLEARANCES HAVE BEEN ARRANGED.

The days of the soapbox speaker in the park and street-corner singers have changed. Besides the fact that both now use cordless microphones, the speaker better have a permit before attracting an audience, and the singers need to know something about copyright law. Even in a free society, you can't just do what you please.

When George Bush was running for president of the United States, his campaign staff liked to lead crowds at rallies in a chorus or two of the popular song of the day "Don't Worry, Be Happy." After a few seconds of the campaign appearance were shown on TV, the song's copyright owners put the Bush campaign on notice: get permission, pay a royalty, or stop using the song. They stopped.

More likely, though, a subject of a publicity campaign will be faced with more minor obstacles, such as getting a permit for the rally in the park, having a section of a sidewalk or street closed for use in an event, or having permission to film or photograph at a library, a school, or some other public building. To proceed without doing so could lead to public embarrassment and a diminishing of whatever positive impression the use of such imagery was intended to convey.

18. ANTICIPATE ANY POTENTIAL NEGATIVE REACTION TO YOUR PUBLICITY EFFORT, AND HAVE A RESPONSE READY.

For decades people who fought with one another in public agreed to follow the Marquis of Queensbury Rules. Alas, in more modern times, rules are off, and despite the threats of lawsuits—indeed, the proliferation of lawsuits—we live in a time of bad manners. People openly launch verbal attacks upon their leaders, competitors, and opponents and just about anyone else they don't like. Cable TV is thick with talk shows that feature people shouting insults at one another and offering candid opinions about brand names, public and private companies, and individuals. It's all in the name of free speech.

TV talk-show host Oprah Winfrey was sued by the cattle industry for comments she made about beef. The issue and the trial was headline news for weeks. Microsoft founder Bill Gates appeared in public and was hit in the face with a cream pie. His Microsoft colleagues, meanwhile, did battle with critics in court and on talk shows over allegations that the company used unfair tactics to create a monopoly in the computer software industry. Furriers, tobacco companies, automobile manufacturers, energy companies, public utilities, candy makers, and even dozens of major media entities, from Disney to Time Warner, find themselves the object of "attack" publicity campaigns.

If you are prepared to take your message to the public—to publicize your subject—be prepared for possible criticism, and even attacks, from pressure groups and special-interest groups as well as from seemingly disinterested parties. The Internet has helped make "sounding off" to a worldwide audience easier than complaining to a handful of strangers in the park. Know this, anticipate what critics may have to say, and have a response ready if one is called for.

19. ESTABLISH BENCHMARKS TO EVALUATE THE SUCCESS OF YOUR
PUBLICITY EFFORT ALONG THE WAY.

There are some very obvious signs that a publicity effort is suc-
ceeding, such as a plethora of print placements, electronic media
appearances, and great crowds at public appearances. But in the
typical, more modest trade or industry-oriented campaign, signs
are not quite so obvious. Market research at various intervals will
indicate if progress is being made. Beyond that, benchmarks to
evaluate success must be constructed, with the written statement
of objectives as the bull's-eye of the target.

For example, if the objective of the publicity campaign is to
increase market share of a product, sales figures recorded before
and at intervals during the program will tell the story. Typically,
putting an offer into a publicity effort is a method of triggering a
response (call for a free guide, a poster, a tape, a booklet, a CD,
tickets, discount coupons, a membership card, etc.).

A "hot line" referenced in articles placed and media appearances provides a monitoring device: check the number of calls.
If there is no measurable increase in contacts during a defined
period, a reevaluation of the strategy and tactics employed is in
order.

20. KNOW WHAT PERCEPTIONS YOUR TARGETED MEDIA HAVE ABOUT YOUR
SUBJECT (AND/OR INDUSTRY).

Many publicists believe that the media are the vehicles to be used
to deliver the subject entity's message, much the way a shipping
company uses trucks. The difference is that trucks go where you
direct them, whereas the media must, in most cases, be *persuaded*
to deliver your message—and, even then, offer no guarantees that
the message will arrive as you had intended. While it is common
to suggest that publicists review research material to know all they
can about their clients, companies, issues, and causes, it is also
worth taking the time to research the media that will be asked to
carry the message to the public.

Most reporters, writers, editors, and producers take their jobs seriously and are reasonably professional. Others are rather open regarding their predisposition, if not their outright bias, for or against various subjects. It is obvious that a publicist trying to promote a cause that might be considered a "liberal" issue—environmental law or cleaner air, for example—would likely not fare well with such magazines as the *Weekly Standard, National Review,* or *American Spectator* or with radio programs such as those of Rush Limbaugh, Oliver North, or G. Gordon Liddy, all aggressively conservative. It is also not uncommon for members of the media to have strong personal feelings about lawyers, the health-care industry, "Wall Street," tobacco, finance, and even publicists.

Know your media. It is certainly a worthy challenge (and part of the job) to change people's minds about your subject. But the first priority of a publicist is to get the message to the most people in the shortest time. To that end, changing people's minds will have to come later. It is probably not in the best interests of your company, client, or cause, in most cases, to devote time to winning over those who are inclined away from your subject. Focus instead on taking your message to professional, open-minded media . . . and building up and out from there.

21. KEEP MEETING REPORTS, A DETAILED LOG, OR A PROJECT JOURNAL.

It is always fashionable to complain about too much paperwork, too many meetings and reports, and too many trees being destroyed to create documents that no one will probably ever read—until something goes wrong. Then the report that notes that the printer agreed to print the envelopes at no cost or that the boss agreed that spouses would travel to the conference at company expense, or that, in fact, it *was* Peabody in Research who insisted the product's name did not mean poison in Dutch—then those pesky reports suddenly are held up as equally valuable as a company car.

The simple everyday fact is that people do not always pay close attention to everything, and people very often remember things differently. A report stored in someone's desk drawer or computer for a reasonable period of time can not only eliminate confusion as to smaller details but also help facilitate future projects or programs by indicating what was decided, rejected, or successful—and who made it work at what cost.

22. DOUBLE-CHECK QUOTES.

Often press releases or story ideas will be rewritten or reworked by members of the media to suit individual styles and fit within a particular context. The one thing that will not be changed is an attributed quote in a release or other material. Whether the quotation offered is your own creation or from Shakespeare, double-check for accuracy and to be sure it clearly makes the point you want to make. It may well be, after the headline, the part of the story that is most remembered or most often repeated.

23. HAVE A RESPONSE MECHANISM IN PLACE FOR COMMENTS.

"People support our efforts overwhelmingly." "This morning alone we received over a hundred calls." Comments such as these not only tell you something about how your publicity effort is going but also provide new information that can be incorporated into the message.

Every day people call or write the White House, the state house, the *New York Times,* NBC, and the makers of Campbell's soup. Whether the public loves what you are doing or hates what you are doing, you should know it. Make it easy for people to find you and register their comments—whether you have solicited them or not. If you are seeking publicity, it is reasonable to assume you want a response, so have the machinery in place.

Include general phone numbers, 800 numbers (or, if charging for the incoming calls, 900 numbers), fax numbers, E-mail addresses, website addresses, or location addresses in your material. It is important not only that the media be able to contact the publicist but also that your constituent groups whose favor you are seeking feel that you want and value their feedback. A successful publicity effort depends on response.

24. BE BRIEF AND CONCISE IN COMMUNICATING TO BOTH THE MEDIA AND THE PUBLIC.

You're busy, and so are the media you are trying to persuade to carry your message. Reporters and editors say the unsolicited caller who wants to warm up the reporter with a few jokes, chat a bit, and then offer "to first tell you something about myself" drives them nuts. While you may very well be an extremely funny and interesting person, the media have only so much time each day to pull together their respective products for presentation. Even quarterly journals still wish to reserve the right to ask you related or background questions *after* they have been convinced that the "hook"—the point of your story that makes the public care to know about it—has been established. So, lead with the hook.

Ask the reporter, the editor, the producer, or whomever if your call is coming at a good time—that is, if the contact has time to listen to a story idea. If they do, get to the point: who, what, when, where, why, and how. If they want to know more, they'll ask. Most likely, even if this is very timely material and approaching deadline—and particularly if the person you are calling doesn't know you—you will be asked to "send something." This something will be your press release, fact sheet, bio, backgrounder, or other pertinent document that the reporter can use to double-check information. This request is pretty standard but has become even more routine with fax machines and E-mail making it possible to respond to the request within seconds.

Your message should be no less concise when going directly to your audience. Major internationally known guests on *The Today Show* or the evening news still get a segment ranging from only 90 seconds to just a few minutes. Seven minutes is considered the longer side of a major talk-show segment. Radio call-in or studio guest opportunities must establish the point of interest—the story hook—in *seconds*. Know what you want to say, make your point, and let the momentum build.

25. Respect the media's time and that of everyone else: get there and/or start on time.

It is one of life's great mysteries why otherwise-intelligent people, who understand that they are supposed to be trying to make a favorable impression and are asking for something (press coverage, attention, support, patronage), take so casual an attitude about keeping people waiting and taking more time than allotted. Arrogance is the curse of the publicist, and arrogance on the part of the publicist's boss or client is the publicist's nightmare.

True, the media may be very interested in what you have to say, but a subject who treats the media (or anyone else in a position to do the subject harm) with disrespect or discourtesy invites unfavorable press—now and/or later—and being marked with the reputation of being difficult to work with, which may adversely affect everything the subject may do in the foreseeable future.

Whether you are meeting a reporter for lunch, holding a press conference, speaking at a function or event, or returning a phone call, a primary rule of professional courtesy (easily as important as the Law of the Jungle or the Code of the West) is: Respect the time of the media and the audience you are hoping will respond favorably to your message.

Show up on time; start on time; finish on schedule. People remember those who do.

26. Know and respect deadlines.

Deadlines are not fluid. With the possible exception of a newsletter you publish yourself and some of the amateurish stuff that passes for publishing on the Internet, publications and programs have set cutoffs by which reporters or producers must file their finished stories so that the fully completed product can be presented to the public at a designated time. In most of the cases worth knowing about, many people are involved in the process, each dependent on others' having done their jobs, to then be able to do his or her own job.

When the press release, phone call, E-mail message, or fax arrives near, at, or past deadline time, the reporter or editor has a right to be angry—whether the media outlet is a daily newspaper, a weekly newsletter, a monthly magazine, radio, or TV. A common first thought is that the reporter or media entity is being duped, and that the material was sent to another media entity much earlier and sent now only in order for the sender to be able to claim that everyone received the story on the same day, when, in fact, someone was given a head start and favored treatment. Usually no such trickery was involved. It's more likely the material's late arrival was the fault of a slow-moving messenger service, slow mail, or a publicist's simply failing to notice the time.

It doesn't matter what the excuse is. The fact is that the material arrived late, and the media person is upset, and this situation does not serve the interests of the publicist or the subject, now or perhaps *ever.*

Perhaps as bad or worse a situation is, after a publicist has worked to generate interest by the media, a designated spokesperson does not show up or call at the agreed time to be interviewed or otherwise provide information. Now the media not only have wasted time but also must use a fallback piece or scramble for a fill-in. In one such instance, the reporter was heard to say, "They had their chance. It'll be a cold day before I write anything about that outfit."

Ouch.

Of course, extenuating circumstances happen all the time (flights canceled, traffic accidents, illness), but all too often the problem is one that could have been averted.

Ignoring or taking a casual attitude regarding media deadlines amounts to sabotaging an opportunity for publicity and, very
often, creates a residual feeling of negativity on the part of a
reporter or editor, leading to bad publicity in the future.

27. KEEP THE MESSAGE SIMPLE.

Whether considering a single press release or an entire publicity
campaign, your public should be able to reflect on your message
and summarize it in a single sentence. Publicists sometimes call this
the *take-away*—the point the audience "takes away" from seeing,
hearing, reading, or considering the subject. At the Lifetime cable
network, the take-away is *". . . television for women."* At CNN's
Headline News network, it's *"a full day's news every 30 minutes."*

Your message can be your company or product's positioning
statement or slogan, as in the two examples noted, but it doesn't
have to be. More often than not, slogans are intended for advertising use and do not convey a theme fitted to a publicity effort. *Did
somebody say McDonald's?* and Nike's *Just do it* anchored two
highly successful ad campaigns, though neither memorable line
offers any sense of the company, the product, or what the public is
supposed to think the line represents.

A press-release headline should provide a concise message
because, quite simply, some editors will determine whether or not
to even read the lead sentence of the release based on their take-
away from the headline.

Whether the target of your message is the media or the public, don't make people work to figure out what you want them to
know.

28. KNOW WHETHER OR NOT FAXES AND E-MAIL TRANSMISSIONS ARE
WELCOMED.

It has been said that in the modern age, people have fewer reasons
than ever to have to talk to each other. Voice mail, answering

machines, faxes, and E-mail permit people to put a personal message on your desk without having to see you or make any personal connection.

These highly efficient systems also have their downside, and publicists should be aware of the negatives. For example, a reporter or editor may have requested that a document of some importance to a work-in-progress be faxed, only to get a call from the source, complaining that the fax number is always busy. If it's busy because the machine is receiving something unsolicited from a publicist who would like to win the reporter's approval, that material had better be pretty hot—because chances are the reporter will be.

To echo the good advice of the telephone company: phone first. A quick call to say that you have a fax to send or would like to send a fax later that day (or even the following day) is a chance for a media contact which could lead to further conversation that might benefit the publicist; it also is a courtesy to the reporter and eliminates the possibility of a hopeful, perhaps very worthy, story idea's being received at a very unwelcome time and getting a poor evaluation.

True, the fax is, to many people, a way of speeding things up, and this added step makes one phone call *two,* taking more time, not less. But remember, technology is swell, but the objective is to make a favorable contact with a media person, with the hope of turning the contact into publicity for your subject. The objective is not to save on phone calls. Try to have your fax get the same reception you would hope to get yourself if you showed up at the reporter's desk.

Regarding E-mail, which is faster and more efficient still, a call ahead might well mean the difference between having your press release or story idea seen and considered or not. Some people report checking their E-mail messages every morning or every afternoon, but this may not be as often as the senders wish.

29. Be aware of the worst things anyone might say or learn about your subject, and have a response ready if it's needed.

It is a reflection of both the intensified media competition and a dramatic lessening of the rules of civility that if there is anything negative, embarrassing, or even mildly controversial about your subject, a publicity effort in which you seek to draw attention to your subject will most likely uncover it.

Virtually every industry, profession, and product category, from bottled water to coffee (both regular and decaf), compact cars to sports utility vans, synthetic fibers or imported cloth, will find special-interest groups waiting to call a press conference to attack its existence. Bad news is regarded as more interesting than good news, so it is not mere cynicism that suggests that an announcement of virtually any appointment will find the person subjected to the utmost scrutiny. Ministers, cabinet officers, teachers, and the new CEO will find their résumés studied for hints of anything colorful or dramatic. A story of a new mall opening will include references to any community resistance to it; coverage of a corporation's 50th-anniversary commemoration is likely to recount any failures, protests, or disasters the company has experienced; a review of the local symphony orchestra's season opening will probably recall the conductor's contract problems or a threatened strike.

Regardless of the subject of your publicity effort, consider anything about it that, if cited by a critic, a competitor, or the media, might derail your program. Prepare a response, and have it in your contingency plans to reference if needed.

In another era, rumors, charges, or outright attacks would have been presented first to the subject of the story for response, defense, or comment. Such has not been the case in modern times, when virtually anything even remotely resembling controversy is rushed to the public, and the subject is forced into a defensive posture. Follow your plan, put your strongest message forward, but again in the words of Mel Brooks, "Hope for the best; expect the worst."

30. STAY FOCUSED ON YOUR SUBJECT, AND DON'T OVERSELL.

Publicity is about getting attention, but it is also about presenting information with which the media and the public may be unfamiliar. Someone once said of a great novelist that once he got into his story, he was mesmerizing, but he insisted on beginning each of his works with "First there was the universe . . ." and presenting so much background information that many readers gave up before getting to the good stuff. Don't provide your audience—the media or the public—with so much information that it challenges people to sort through what you've said to find the essential subject material. Your backgrounders, brochures, fact sheets, bios, reports, and other supporting material can be offered and made available, but the essential method, whether in a press release, an interview, a speech, or a handout, should be clear, concise, and so to the point that there is no doubt about what you want people to take away from your presentation.

In a related vein, don't overpromise, exaggerate, or inflate claims. This will distract from the subject and may cause the audience to question the credibility of your message. If that occurs, not only have you missed the opportunity to win them over, but also you'll have to work even harder to reengage them for a second try.

31. BE PREPARED TO HANDLE RESPONSES AND REQUESTS (WITH ADEQUATE PHONE LINES, FAXES, COMPUTER TERMINALS, AND PERSONNEL).

This is not the same as having a mechanism for response (23); it is about effective follow-through and turning a mechanism into an opportunity. Several comedians have variations on the joke about calling "911" to report an emergency and becoming upset over being put on hold, but at least they got to listen to the new Yanni album while they waited.

People who are responding to a publicity effort and are calling to provide or request information, make a reservation, or pledge support are annoyed, if not totally turned off, over either getting a busy signal, having the phone go unanswered, hearing a recording that says to call back at another time (that is more convenient for the owner of the phone number), or being put on hold.

A prerecorded list of endless telephone options (press "1" to be put on hold; press "2" to hear more about what you can do while we have you on hold, etc.) is equally annoying. Even worse are "hot lines"—their very name suggesting an earnest responsiveness—going unanswered, being busy, or presenting prerecorded messages that convey less than a sense of being "hot."

Some publicists might say that having more of a reaction or response to their efforts than they can handle is the kind of problem they'd like to have.

It's not.

When people can't get through to you, they tell other people about it. It is human nature to share or to vent one's frustrations or irritations. A potential "support call" could end up in the negative column. If the point is to make more people aware and positive about the subjects, the more positives and fewer negatives registered, the better. Of course everything can't always be perfect all the time, but consider offering apologies in advance if lines are busy, and an incentive to keep trying, even if it is only to be put on a mailing list to receive something at a later date.

32. Update contact lists frequently.

It is said that telephone directories are out-of-date by the time they are printed; that it is simply the nature of things—people move around. That may be an unfortunate fact of life for the phone company, but it cannot be for publicists. A press release directed to a reporter, a columnist, an editor, or a producer who has moved up, on, or out can convey an impression that the publicist doesn't care enough to stay on top of the matter or, worse, doesn't track the publication, program, or other venue regularly enough to know who's in and who's out.

Addressing people by name is a way of showing respect. Addressing something to "editor" or "producer" or to someone no longer associated with the enterprise is a sign of unprofessionalism, sloppiness, or laziness.

33. KNOW IF YOUR MESSAGES HAVE BEEN RECEIVED.

You have painstakingly prepared your press release, double-checked facts and quotes, issued your media alerts, fine-tuned your list, and faxed, messengered, and E-mailed what just may be the most dramatic and stunning announcement of the year, which anyone in his or her right mind would think deserved the broadest possible coverage. Now what?

Publicists are salespeople, and as any good salesperson knows, you don't just sit and wait for the phone to ring. It is another step, and it takes time, but while "phone first" is a good idea, "phone *again*" is a better and sometimes much more necessary one.

Do not assume that your communications have been received just because you sent them. E-mail messages do not always get read promptly. Faxes have been known to pile up at the machine before being collected, delivered, or read. Messenger services encounter heavy traffic and, alas, sometimes accidentally deliver to a wrong address—where it can take hours to correct a mistake, if it is corrected at all. Don't just sit waiting and hoping and watching the newswires.

It may not be necessary to call everyone on your list every time, but certainly on your most important communications to your most influential media, a call to make sure the material has been received is worth the time and trouble.

34. Make certain that your budget includes the costs of
long-distance calls, faxes, messenger service, Federal Express,
and postage stamps.

Whether a large corporation, a trade association, a private practice, a small business, or a street musician (OK, maybe not a street
musician), you don't want to go over budget on your publicity
program, and by the very nature of what you are doing, it could
happen. Messenger-service deliveries for a single press release
could run into hundreds of dollars, and several press releases per
year can add up. If you are on the West Coast or in the southeast
part of the United States, phone calls and faxes to the financial
press in New York City can amount to a significant expense. These
expenses can be difficult to estimate in order to prepare a budget
in advance and often are listed simply as "miscellaneous expense"
and are very underestimated.

One suggested way of estimating such costs is to review the
names on your media list and create a "profile," noting how often
a typical name on the list is likely to be called, faxed, messengered, and/or written to during the period of the publicity push.
Estimate the cost of servicing that one name and multiply it by the
number of names on the list.

It is not an exact or perfect figure, but it will at least provide
a better estimate than picking numbers for postage or phone calls
based on previous budgets which may or may not be representative of future projects. It also beats going over budget or sending
the client an unbudgeted bill for phones, fax, and Fed Ex that
amounts to several thousand dollars annually.

35. Know the form and means by which the most important media
on your list prefer to receive material.

Be as creative as you care to be with brochures, annual reports, and
audio- and videotapes, but when it comes to press releases, follow
the standard form: use 8½" × 11" paper, typed double-spaced; list

the contact's name and phone numbers; use a concise headline; begin the text with a dateline; limit the length to one or two pages. Additional information and details can be provided in accompanying backgrounders and fact sheets or upon request. Remember that graphics and artwork can fill in and lose a lot of their intended artistic appeal after the photocopier or fax machine has had a crack at them. Different media will have different *preferred* specifications, but this form is recognized as standard.

The question arises often of how to know in what form, or by what means of delivery, the media would like to receive material. The answer is: You ask them.

While numerous directories list how the *New York Times,* the *Wall Street Journal,* the *Chicago Tribune,* the Associated Press, *Time, Newsweek,* and other major media outlets prefer to receive press releases and other material, the best way to make certain you are giving them what they want is to ask. Some are insistent on limiting the length of faxes they will accept; others prefer electronic transmissions. Some require longer lead times than others. Certain trade publications—especially legal and medical it seems—understandably want vastly more in the way of details than most other media. In these cases the "Limit it to one to two pages" rule is off. When in doubt, ask.

36. FOLLOW UP AND FOLLOW THROUGH.

Making contact with members of the media is how publicists typically bring the message of their subjects to the larger public, whether that is a trade audience, the general public, or a specifically targeted group. But few successful media placements result from a single contact. Even the most experienced publicists, working with members of the media they have known for years— where such considerations as credibility, ethics, and trust were resolved long ago—will routinely find that selling a story idea, an interview, or the covering of an event is arranged over several phone calls or meetings.

A first contact regarding a subject typically ends with the reporter's requesting, or the publicist's promising to send, a write-up on the subject. The material is sent. Another contact determines whether or not it was received and if there are any questions. More conversations will take place. Sometimes, when all the parties are known and the media are familiar with the subjects, the process may be shorter, although it is not uncommon to hear a publicist say, "I've been working on this one for months." It is through this process as well that publicists have an opportunity to build on their media relationships—or build them at all.

37. MAKE CERTAIN THAT THE MEDIA CONTACT LISTED CARES ABOUT YOUR SUBJECT.

To put it simply, don't waste your own time and that of the writer, reporter, columnist, editor, producer, or booker when the person you really want to talk with is seated one desk or office away. A brief phone call that determines the interest (or lack thereof) may be prefaced or followed with a simple comment such as, "You may not be the one I should be talking with about this . . ."

That comment is usually followed by an offer to listen to the idea or a suggestion to call _____.

Within media organizations, as in other organizations, people move around, change departments, and move on. It is important not only that media lists are kept current to reflect such moves, but also that the names on the list are still the people who want what you have to offer.

38. KNOW HOW OFTEN TO CALL MEMBERS OF THE MEDIA—AND HOW OFTEN *NOT* TO CALL.

Persistence is one of the salesperson's attributes—not giving up. As a salesperson, the publicist must appreciate that there are many more story ideas being pitched than there is room or time to print or broadcast. Once an idea has been presented, material sent, the follow-up call made . . . then what?

Call again. Don't assume that, because the right steps have been followed, the story is under consideration. It might be, but it might also be spiked. Call again and ask if any additional information is needed. Have another angle on the story ready to offer if needed, perhaps an updated detail or two that will make the story more timely or tie it to a current news hook.

And if there is still no commitment to use the story, smile and move on. Take the story somewhere else. As Burt Bacharach and Hal David wrote so poignantly, "Knowing when to leave can be the hardest thing that anyone can learn." The song's message is a useful one. Don't jeopardize a relationship with a member of the media who may be valuable to you at a future date. Even Michael Jordan knows that you don't win every game. Fortunately, there are enough media options—particularly in cable—that a story idea turned down doesn't have to mean the story's dead.

The great challenge is for the publicist to learn how to take a pulse. When does the publicist cross the line from being professionally persistent to becoming a pain in the rear end? It's not after three calls or ten; it's when the *feeling* tells you it is time to say, "Thanks anyway," and move on. Experience teaches. Be sensitive to the media person's tone of voice, and listen to the words. Sometimes "I'm thinking about it" means no. Listen for it, and don't be afraid to let the person off the hook by simply asking, "If you don't think this is going to happen, do you have a problem with my taking it to someone else?" That should most likely force a decision and move the story along.

39. ANTICIPATE QUESTIONS, AND INCLUDE ANSWERS IN YOUR PUBLICITY MATERIALS.

Keep it simple; be concise, but anticipate what the first question would be that a reporter or producer might ask after reviewing your material. Stick first to *who, what, when, where, why,* and *how,* but know that it is all right to provide a bit of color and some additional fact, such as the number of years the subject has been around, any awards or other recognition received, or any particular distinction associated to individuals quoted in your material. This additional data can be in the press release, backgrounder, bios, fact sheets—just so it is *there*.

40. LIST CONTACTS BY NAME AND TITLE.

Names on your media list should be of people, not just titles. It is true that some media organizations prefer to have material sent to the "news desk" or "assignment editor" because the people in those positions often serve on a rotating basis with other staffers. But that doesn't mean that you cannot maintain a list of names of people who you know follow your subject and with whom you should stay in regular contact. It is an advantage to the publicist to talk with someone who already has some understanding or frame of reference for the subject, rather than pitching to yet another person who may or may not be interested. Another piece of advice from the wisdom of salespeople: If you want to sell something to the organ grinder, don't waste your time talking with the monkey.

41. USE FACT SHEETS AND BACKGROUNDERS TO PROVIDE DETAILS.

There are more things that you will want to say about your subject, and more that the media will want to know, than belong in a press release. Remember that the press release should read as if it could be inserted into a newspaper or magazine and appear to have been written by an objective reporter trying to bring information to the public. While a columnist or feature writer may "rave" about a subject, a reporter should just stick to the facts—and so should the press release.

But in keeping with the guidelines of telling who, what, when, where, why, and how in not more than 500 words, a fact sheet or a backgrounder included with the press release or in the press kit, or as a helpful piece of research prior to an interview or a speech, provides the information that didn't fit the space or format of the release. This includes such information as a subject's history; organizational structure; noteworthy items of importance or significance, such as a review of stock performance, management changes, or past policy decisions that affected the subject's financial status; the roles of important support people and support systems; and forecasts.

Backgrounders and fact sheets are not ads. Ads can appropriately be included in press kits, along with sales brochures and promotional pieces, but you should maintain a strict distinction between promotional and informational communications vehicles.

42. PREPARE FOR INTERVIEWS, AND PREPARE INTERVIEWERS WITH
BACKGROUND MATERIAL IN ADVANCE.

Preparation for interviews is an exercise that is often glossed over and disregarded. Shy, nervous, or inexperienced interview subjects—even at the CEO level—can become rattled or intimidated prior to an interview and can be so guarded, anxious, or even overprepared that the interview conveys a staged, insincere feeling that can be represented negatively in press accounts. Other interview subjects may be so confident, glib, and comfortable with their subjects that they choose to "wing it" and present a sense of detachment and aloofness that can be interpreted any number of ways, few of them positive.

Obviously, neither example is likely to result in a good impression being made, a good presentation of or by the subject, or any favorable publicity coming out. The interview subject who, on advice of the legal department, has been given a list of subjects about which the comment must be "No comment" also doesn't help the cause. The style of the presentation is often every bit as important as the substance of the presentation.

Of course, some people are shy and are in fact truly "not good with people." When these people are in positions of responsibility and authority, it is as physically and emotionally upsetting to them to be interviewed as it is bad for the company, product, cause, or event they are supposed to be publicizing.

But the purpose of this book is not to suggest ways for people to overcome shyness; rather, it is to offer recommendations to effectively publicize a subject. One approach is to team up the shy or uneasy (or humorless or outright dull, if brilliant) person with someone who will represent that person's counterpart, much the way a discussion group uses a moderator. A good moderator makes his or her guests look good and doesn't overshadow or upstage, effectively remaining a facilitating, background presence, suggesting a word here, a thought there, and an occasional point of information, and gently steering the conversation back to—or away from—a given area.

An experienced public relations person can usually fill the moderator's role. And the media explanation of the staging? Honesty is the best policy: simply note that the individual who is the appropriate source of the information is only too willing to meet with the media but is very uncomfortable in such situations, so to keep things moving, the PR person is going to sit in. If the media person has a problem with that, it's the media person's problem to deal with. Ground rules for interviews are set all the time, and it is quite appropriate to do so, if you feel you need to.

Still, a walk-through, covering subjects likely to be discussed in the interview and what forms or examples the answers should take, is both appropriate and important.

Similarly, the confident interview subject who wants to "wing it" should be reminded that there may very well be no makeup exams here, no second chances to recover if the interview goes badly. To that end, as in the previous example, a walk-through to review material likely to be discussed is in everyone's best interests.

A packet of information should be delivered to the interviewer at least a day in advance. It may be only the press kit with backgrounders, bios, fact sheets, and any timely pertinent information that could come up in the interview, such as recent studies, position papers, or reports of controversy. In any case, by having the interviewer and the subject both reviewing the same background material just prior to the session, the framework or context of the interview will be the same for both parties.

Will there be unexpected questions? If the interviewer is good, yes. The publicist should help prepare the subject for such possibilities, as well as prepare a list of points that the subject should try to smoothly insert into the conversation. Being prepared is important. Pausing and considering how a remark will look in print before responding to a question can be critical.

43. Ask for feedback.

All too often, in both the planning and implementation stages of a publicity program, the principals operate in a vacuum. That is, even with research in hand, they communicate only with one another, failing to effectively challenge the points they are trying to advance and, therefore, often being broadsided and taken aback by comments that had not been anticipated.

Anticipate them. Test your plan. Ask for feedback. Research and polling services will provide good evaluations that will test the public's response to your message in discreet sample groups. Once the message is out—through a speech, an interview, an announcement, or a press release—gauge the immediate reaction of the media by *asking them* for a reaction to what you've presented. Then, be prepared to react. If your message raises unanticipated questions, formulate a response.

In most cases, publicity efforts are positive announcements aimed at generating interest for something also positive—a product, a service, a company, a trade group, an event, or a cause—and controversy will not likely be a factor. But as controversy seems ever present in media situations, preparation is your best defense.

44. Find the element of your subject that connects with your audience on a personal level; define it, and stay "on message."

The story is often told of the sign in the "Clinton for President" campaign office that read: It's the economy, stupid. People may debate for a long time whether or not the word "stupid" was actually necessary, but the campaign manager's point was that, as the workers spread out to carry the candidate's message, the opposition would be trying to raise issues touching on morality, religion, personal choice, militarism, racial quotas, and more. The Clinton people felt that the most powerful, emotional, and meaningful message was one to which every voter could relate on a personal level: how economic conditions touched family living every day. Food costs, health-care costs, the cost of education, personal income, savings, and even the price of a gallon of gas were everybody's business. The economy.

Whatever else that particular campaign revealed, its analysts believed that their candidate understood and related better to something to which a majority of voters could relate. And they stayed focused on it.

This is the fundamental challenge to the publicist:

- Find a point relating to your subject that will be most relevant to your audience—the issue of *what's in it for them?*
- Stay focused on that point throughout the phases of your effort.

The constant tendency of a publicist and his or her company or client is to be pulled back to the subject in ways that it relates to the company or client. Remember that the audience may give you the courtesy of its attention and perhaps even a smile, but whether or not people buy, subscribe to, enlist in, embrace, or support your subject will be based on how they can relate to it on their own personal terms.

45. Double-check financial information—and then check it again.

This point may require the least explanation of any. When trying to generate attention and awareness, pretty much nothing short of a homicide conviction will throw the effort off-course like showing a misplaced comma or decimal point. A mistake in numbers,

The Complete Guide to Publicity

whether an error in proposed cost or projected income or the most inadvertent typo, can blunt credibility and trust, two essential ingredients in achieving good publicity. Check and recheck financial data in press releases, reports, and fact sheets. To many in your audience, the financial information is the only information that counts.

46. Do not go off the record. Do not go off the record. *Do not go off the record.*

In the old movies, when someone went "off the record" with the media, the statement implied total trust, protection of anonymity, and security. In modern times, even if some reporters are still willing to go to jail to protect a source, the system is sufficiently flawed that "leaks" (the revealing of otherwise confidential or privileged information), tapes, wiretaps, eavesdropping, and the driving ambition of the window washer to land a lucrative book contract have compromised all that was once protected by antiquated terms such as "honor" and "a gentlemen's agreement."

No matter how comfortable or trusting your relationship with members of the media may have become, there is only one rule to follow here: *If you don't want to see it in print, don't say it.*

47. Ask the members of the media if there are any more questions.

Of the many press conferences held on a routine basis—by world leaders, sports figures, entertainers, people of science and the arts—nearly all begin with a carefully worded prepared statement. Yet, if any part of the press conference makes it to the evening news or the next day's paper, it is a spontaneous answer to a pointed question. The carefully worded statement that the publicist might hope would be what people take away from the press conference is virtually ignored and forgotten in reaction to something more dramatic and deemed worthy of public attention. Don't let an opportunity pass you by.

48. CHECK IN ADVANCE IF ANY OF YOUR MOST IMPORTANT MEDIA TARGETS
HAVE SPECIAL REQUIREMENTS.

For many years the standard publicity photograph was a black-and-white 8" × 10" glossy print. Most media will still accept that, but advances in processing have both relaxed and altered the rules of acceptability. Many newspapers and magazines not only will now accept color photographs but also prefer them. Some print media will not accept studio portrait or "posed" photographs, insisting that the subject be in a natural environment.

Television once discouraged wearing white on the air and encouraged light blue in its place. Color TV cameras now have no problem with white, though operators are careful about pointing a camera at "reflective" colors and fabrics.

Publicists taking recordings along to TV or radio appearances will find that the control room or engineer's "board" looks impressive and as if it could control air traffic . . . but it might not be able to play a record (anymore). Tape cartridges likewise may or may not be standard commercial cassette formats.

As more options are available, it is wise to have a basic standard press kit with black-and-white photos and 8½" × 11" paper for most of the contacts on your list, but for your "hottest" media list entries—those likely to reach the largest audience or having the greatest influence on your target audience—before sending material (wasting money and having to retrace your steps), inquire as to which formats they are prepared to accept or would prefer. Publicists have arrived at television studios with "a great piece of tape" only to find that the format of the tape was either not one the studio was equipped to play or just not the format preferred.

A publicist needs to look professional, act professionally, and maintain good relationships with media people for future projects. As with the audience at large, a good strategy is to give them what they want.

49. KNOW THE LEAD TIMES OF THE MEDIA ON YOUR LIST, AND MAKE
CERTAIN THESE DATES WORK WITH YOUR STRATEGY.

Daily newspapers and the immediacy of TV or radio are not a problem for you. A problem is when you want to reach air travelers and decide the best vehicle for your message is the many wonderfully colorful, slick in-flight magazines that air travelers read in a leisurely setting at times of relaxed susceptibility. You pitch your story ideas to several in-flight publications, and they all agree to accept them. This is a problem because your employer or client needs these stories to appear *now*—and the lead time for these publications is typically four months to a year.

Just as knowing deadlines is important, understanding the lead times of each media contact on your list is important, particularly as it applies to the timeline part of your plan. How soon your publicity must appear in order to achieve your objectives must determine the choice of media you approach at any given stage.

Often a reporter, an editor, or a producer of a daily publication or program will write or tape a story on your subject and advise you that he or she has no idea when it will run. Many publicists have found that to be an understatement. A press release sent to a daily trade paper was received, and the editor told the publicist that he would "do something with it." He did. A story incorporating much of the release's information ran in the publication . . . in February—nearly five months later.

This example is a somewhat extreme case, but not by much. In the follow-up calls after issuing a press release or upon hearing that a story idea you pitched has been accepted, or following an interview, be sure to ask when the story is going to run. Sometimes media people can answer specifically; other times you can get a general idea, such as "sometime next week." Use this information to help you coordinate and maximize the impact of the publicity you are seeking with what you know you are getting.

50. Consider the effect of your competition on your
publicity plan.

An *ad* is yours to say whatever you want however you want—and
to leave *out* whatever you want. You don't have to say that someone
else has, or is doing, what amounts to the essence of your message—or has been doing it longer and, perhaps, at a lower cost. You
also don't have to say that *Consumer Reports* or another rating service found yours to be a very well run operation and went on to
include you among the ten best in your field: *eighth,* to be exact.
You don't have to say any of this because it is, after all, *your ad.*

But publicity is not advertising. When you take your story to
the media, they are likely to include such information and more.
In a perfect world you wouldn't have to worry. Your audience
would know you, love and respect you, support you, and rate you
tops in customer-satisfaction surveys. But the media reside in an
imperfect world and very often feel obliged to be objective and tell
both sides of a story.

You may not have to worry about this. Your image and the
range and depth of your subject may be enough to keep the focus
totally on you. But just in case, consider the position of your subject relative to your competition, and anticipate what might be
said about your subject or against it or how it might be characterized in any negative way. Include a reference in your material
(brochure or fact sheet) that addresses this, as a preemptive measure against critics.

51. Be realistic regarding your publicity expectations.

It is important to set objectives, but it is just as important to be
realistic. "Generate a higher profile and greater awareness and
recognition" is a perfectly legitimate and manageable objective, but
"Get the cover of *Time, Newsweek, Forbes,* or *Fortune*" is on the
level of "Win the lottery" to most subjects. Publicists should be
honest with their employers and clients about what can realistically

be achieved with the media and what cannot. Agencies are fired every day for "overpromising" or for not fulfilling what the client *understood to be* a promise to deliver something widely regarded as unattainable. A good plan, a good subject, and a lot of energy can "generate a higher profile and greater awareness and recognition" without disappointing the client or the boss. Don't promise to deliver what is not necessary to have anyway.

52. DISTINGUISH BETWEEN A NEWS RELEASE, A PRESS RELEASE, AND A FEATURE STORY.

As years have gone by, standards have relaxed, and there may be only a handful of "sticklers" remaining who believe that a *news* release should be information that qualifies as news.

One entity acquiring another, or two entities merging, the introduction of a new product, the first announcement of a major event to be held, a new record set for something noteworthy, and a major discovery—whether it is a cure for a disease or a previously unreleased recording by Elvis Presley or the Beatles—are all examples of news.

United Airlines serving Starbucks coffee on its flights is worthy of a *press* release, but it is not news. Ditto the fact that your office will be closed the day before Christmas. Thank you for sharing the information, but it doesn't qualify as news.

Releases that begin with sentences such as "Have you ever wondered how many toothbrushes an average family goes through in a year?" or "Jaoquin wondered why, despite his being the only lute maker in the village, business was slow" should be neither a news release nor a press release. Those are feature stories.

Yet, in attempting to generate publicity, too many publicists erase the lines and treat all three types of information as if they were equal in their newsworthiness. This suggestion of a total absence of the ability to recognize what is news and what is not is a reason some editors who take their work seriously lose respect for publicists and public relations practitioners.

Like the story of the boy who playfully cried "Wolf!" so often that when a wolf actually attacked him, his cries were ignored because everyone thought he was just joking again, the publicist who insists on issuing "news releases" for items of secondary importance will come to be, if not ignored, then certainly not taken seriously for having either much in the way of news judgment or anything important to say at all.

Whichever of the three you're actually trying to put out, remember:

- No exclamation points!
- News should be newsworthy.

53. BE HONEST IN TERMS OF YOUR "MESSAGE CONTENT."

To the guideline "be concise, be brief, be accurate," we now add *be honest.* While it seems as if this directive should be so obvious as to not need repeating, the reality is that everyone faces an irresistible temptation to exaggerate and "to take certain liberties" when it comes to publicizing a subject that has great personal significance or importance.

Rein it in. The media and the public are so inundated with spun information and self-serving data that a barrier now exists, and much of what is said is discounted. To take a bit of liberty with a sacred phrase: the presumption too often is that a publicist is lying until proven innocent. Do not embellish your message so much, at a time when you are seeking a higher profile, that your audience discounts or rejects what you have to say.

54. KEEP ACCURATE, CURRENT FILES OF WHAT YOU HAVE SUPPLIED TO THE MEDIA, AND IF AND HOW IT HAS BEEN USED.

You cannot adequately gauge the effectiveness of your effort (during or at the completion of a wave of publicity activity) if you don't monitor if and how what you have sent out to the media has been used. If the most common complaint among publicists is that material sent out was not used, or that the material was "mis-represented" or someone was misquoted—if he or she was quoted at all—you need to know this and analyze what happened.

The first step is to ask selected (influential) members of the media if they are receiving your material. If the answer is no, add the person to the list. If the answer is yes, then try to determine why the material is not being used (*asking* is a good way to start). This may be the time for self-analysis and for modifying the materials used or the approach taken.

55. DEFINE THE SUBJECT OF YOUR PUBLICITY EFFORT: A PERSON, A PRODUCT, A COMPANY, AN ASSOCIATION, AN ISSUE, OR A CAUSE.

Some people have been waiting a long time for the world to hear their story. They've already rehearsed the interview and seen the story in their minds. Many exchanges with staff, customers, clients, supporters, and friends have made them at ease enough with their subject that, when the opportunity for publicity arrives, they speak comfortably and confidently, as if they are addressing an educated audience who is as familiar with the subject as they are themselves. This is not a good approach.

If there is little or no public awareness of your subject, it is important that the public come away with a clear idea of what you need it to know. Think of how many times you have heard broadcasters begin a brief recap of a discussion with the phrase "For those of you who are just joining us . . ." Assume your audience is just joining you. Don't create an information overload by putting too many names of people or products into your press release; don't speak in interviews or briefings as if your audience already knows who you are and what you are talking about. Keep it simple and focused.

For those who feel they've been around long enough that everyone *should* know who they are and what they want, that is a risky assumption to make if you hope to get the maximum benefit from your publicity effort. As an example, consider how many times Donald Trump is seen commenting in the media. Many people in the public would say he gets a lot of publicity. But is it publicity for one or all of his hotels? His casinos? Real estate developments? Books? Airline? Is it just that he has become such a celebrity that every time he appears in print or on TV, all of his various enterprises benefit from the publicity? Or suffer from it? Are there numbers of people who see him being interviewed at a prize fight or restaurant opening—clearly wanting to be noticed, seeking publicity—and asking who *is* this guy?

A community hospital invited a number of celebrities from different fields to appear at its new facility during its Grand Opening week. The events were hugely successful. But did the public understand that they were being lured to the appearances to see *the facility* or to see the celebrities?

Unless the ultimate objective is only to see your (or your client's or your boss's) name and photograph in the media, stay focused on your subject, define it, and don't leave your public with any doubt about why you wanted them to know about your subject.

56. Determine the level and focus of your message in terms of its "newsworthiness."

Just as you must weigh the newsworthiness of your subject message in terms of designating it a news release, a press release, or a feature story, it is similarly important to categorize your subject to appropriately target your *media*. That is to say, just as there are feature stories, there are feature media: publications and programs that are totally absent of hard news. Collectors' publications; fashion and hairstyle magazines, TV shows, and videos; and exercise and fitness programs are examples of non-news feature media that are influential to their respective audiences. Magazines such as *Forbes' American Heritage, Natural History,* and *Civilization* are examples of publications that take a "harder" look at their subject matter, yet still are feature oriented, rather than hard news or trade. The *Wall Street Journal,* on the other hand, despite its random articles of a lighter nature, is regarded as anything but a feature-oriented publication.

By defining your subject's *niche,* you better define and narrow the list of media that will likely be more advantageous to your effort.

57. WHENEVER POSSIBLE, USE VISUALS.

The most commonly heard comment after favorably reviewing an annual report is "It looks good." That is often a very literal description of people's opinions. Far more people *look* at annual reports than *read* annual reports.

The same is true of magazine and newspaper articles that feature photographs, charts, or other graphic material. Television producers would prefer videotape or film to accompany each story but will settle for even still photographs, recognizing that an audience's interest is attracted and sustained far more by anything visual than audio and print text combined.

Speakers know that slides, photos, charts, and graphs enhance presentations and hold audience interest. Choosing one or more visuals to accompany a press release or other print information will greatly increase the media's interest in using the material. The better the visuals (more interesting, technically and graphically well executed, reflective of substantive information), the greater the likelihood of the material's gaining greater media and audience interest.

58. CONSIDER THE TIMELINESS OF YOUR SUBJECT; EDITORS AND PRODUCERS WILL.

Experienced publicists scour the day's news for anything happening that they can in any way relate to their subjects and issue press releases or media alerts in order to gain publicity and advance their causes. This is one reason the public so frequently sees and hears the same "experts" commenting on the day's events—even if the events from one day to the next are of the most diverse nature. It is not as much the media's calling upon these individuals as it is the individuals' volunteering their comments to the media. The resulting exposure affords an opportunity, if only in an introduction, to publicize whatever the speaker's particular focus is (a book, a film, a cause, or identification with a particular event, institution, or profession).

Obviously the publicist hopes that circumstances favor the timing of the subject for which the publicity is sought, but the publicist also knows that opportunities can be created and that timeliness can be "borrowed." For example:

- The opening of a new health and fitness center sometime after the wave had crested and the "fitness craze" was on the downslope. The publicist might position the new center as being for the "survivors" of the trend, people who are serious about their subject and therefore worth knowing about, now that the amateurs and dabblers have gone back to the coffee bars.
- A hospital or medical practice publicizes its current market positioning of its services as being a response to heightened public concern about public health care—even if it means beginning a press release with: "Last year the public received some shocking news about health care. Today, a solution . . ."

Editors and producers will look for an element of timeliness in the subject presented—after all, they like to think of what they do as "news"—but the publicist can find that news *hook,* and that will embrace either a timeliness or a sufficient level of interest, importance, or value as to make the timing factor irrelevant.

59. ORCHESTRATE YOUR USE OF PUBLICITY PHOTOS.

Subjects with accompanying visual material are regarded as both more interesting and more likely to be used and remembered, and photographs are the most versatile, effective, and dramatic of the visuals. A graph or chart may show some startling comparisons or ranges, but people like to see pictures of people and of scenes to which they can relate. Photos also allow the publicist the opportunity to stretch interest and keep revisiting the same factual material with fresh, updated, or interestingly different photographs.

A theatrical production may run for months, but each week, with or without an accompanying press release, a new and different photograph showing a different scene or performer, the producer or director, or work going on behind the scenes can inform the audience of something about the production that it may not have noticed before.

Any subject that can be photographed—a school, a service organization, a practice, an event, a product, a candidate, an athlete, an entertainer—can be photographed from numerous angles and distances, and the resulting work, unlike the text version of the message, can be presented to the media with frequency, at whatever intervals the plan allows (the candidate at different locations, for example, or the product being used by different people in a variety of settings). A well-orchestrated release of a series of interesting images can increase both the volume and the longevity of a publicity effort.

60. Determine to what degree you can create "photo opportunities" for your subject.

The phrase "photo opportunity" has become an accepted term in publicity, rarely meaning to actually take advantage of an opportunity, but rather to create an event or scene worthy of a publicity photo: an entertainer meeting an athlete, a starlet posing at a landmark, children using a product, and so on. Practically any scene that can be conceived, staged, and photographed, and can qualify under the term "visual interest," can be incorporated into a publicity effort.

Be creative and imaginative, but recognize that editors and producers, while aware that an interesting photo can have news value and appeal, tend to take particular note of publicists who contrive and create news for publicity purposes ("synthetic" news) and, alas, then discount or question the integrity of the subject's more legitimate successes.

61. KNOW WHAT, IF ANY, POLICIES OR STANDARDS YOUR MOST IMPORTANT MEDIA TARGETS HAVE FOR PHOTOGRAPHS.

Most media have their own guidelines for the types of photos they will accept. Big-city daily papers will accept standard black-and-white photos of an event and its principals for feature stories or the business section, but major news stories typically require exclusive photos by an assigned photographer or wire-service photos. At the other extreme, the many cable TV channels have so much time to fill that they have been known to use live telephone interviews and virtually put a passport photo up on the screen.

Since the whole point of generating a publicity effort is to create the best possible impression, send only quality photos with your information, and double-check which media will accept color or demand exclusivity. A good reason to inquire about standards is to avoid sending material that is totally unsuitable for the format, thus appearing unprofessional for not having checked first.

62. KNOW THE IMPORTANCE OF A PUBLICITY PHOTO CAPTION.

In the instances noted in the examples, such as the ongoing theater production, for which a series of photos can be disseminated over the run of the show, it is not necessary to send the accompanying press release each time, as the release is already in the media files, and running frequent scenes does not mean getting stories written all the time. Usually, the feeling is that the photo is enough. This means the photo caption has added importance. It must not only describe the action taking place in the photo but also convey a sense of the show (comedy, drama, family show), identify persons shown in the photo, and perhaps mention as well the show's writers or director.

By their nature, captions need to be short, so the publicist is faced with the challenge of saying a lot in a few words. Keep in mind as well that, even if a story accompanies the photo, the photo may still be all a segment of the audience will skim, making the caption even more central to your effort.

Identifying persons shown in photos is important, as is double-checking the correct spelling of names, as well as getting signed releases to use the photos. With the exception of public figures, individuals have the right to demand that their distinguishable likenesses (photos) not be used without their permission. This means that signed releases are not required for persons shown in crowd scenes where no one individual is recognizable. Even in the case of public figures, original photos or even "official" photos may typically not be used without permission for commercial purposes, such as an implied endorsement. Be concise; be thorough; be aware of legal rights and restrictions; make the photo reflect the subject.

63. Make photographs interesting.

While it may seem obvious or unnecessary to remind publicists that photos used for publicity purposes should be "interesting," too many photos are released that are of poor quality or that feature an obviously staged or cliché pose. Remember that the point of having a photograph included with media information is to convey a positive image—to make a good impression. Photos should be clear and sharp, no reproduction beyond a second-generation copy, and should be flattering to the subject. Avoid fake poses with telephones. Photos showing people in motion, doing what they do, are more interesting than posed photos of people smiling and looking directly into the camera.

64. Try to make your photographs "speak for themselves."

Not *every* picture is worth a thousand words. Relate your photo to the subject you are publicizing. A new product introduction should probably show the product's inventor or the head of a company holding the product or standing before a large representation of it, just as the announcement of a new real estate development might show the developers with a scale model of the project.

A photo of a CEO on the phone, addressing a group around a conference table, or getting out of a car and smiling would not be one that spoke to the subject of the photo, nor would a stock, studio-portrait shot support the message in the strongest way. Many executives and others who do not like being photographed believe that once they've posed for the authorized company photo, that should be enough. It's not. Very often that is exactly the type of uninteresting photograph the media will *not* use.

65. Limit the number of people in a publicity photo.

Unless your subject is a choir, an orchestra, or the Corleone Family wedding picture, limit the number of people in each photograph. Group scenes where many people have to squeeze into the frame do not support a good publicity effort. A picture should tell a story, and the story should be more than a sea of faces. There are exceptions. The supreme court of the United States, the Chicago Bulls, and your board of directors each require a group photograph in the press kit or the annual report, but for publicity purposes, focusing on individuals and groups of no more than five people to a photo offers a less distracting, potentially more interesting scene and story.

Scenes of movement or activity (people engaged in doing what they do) are more interesting than posed stares into the camera, but having too many people in a photo diminishes the focus on the subject and draws attention to individual features, for better or worse. The most effective and widely used publicity photographs keep the emphasis on the subject.

66. "Frame" or crop your publicity photos so that your image/subject is centered and background and peripheral interests do not distract.

Stay focused on the subject. It is often tempting to include elements of visual interest that appear in the frame—beautiful scenery or attractive supporters—but too frequently audience members' eyes will be drawn to the strikingly good-looking (or somewhat disheveled) person behind or near a speaker. Microphone cords and empty chairs that draw the viewers' eyes away from the subject do not belong in publicity photos. Flowers or trees that provide a beautiful background or frame in a live appearance, can look as if they are growing out of someone's head in a photo.

67. Remember the purpose and importance of publicity photos when planning your budget.

Publicity photographs should be taken by professional photographers. These are not vacation slides. The success of the product, company, service, event, or whatever the subject of your effort may depend in large part on the impression you make. Photographs are a major part of that impression. Compare the fees of professional photographers whose work you admire or know to be effective. It is easy to hear a fee quoted and be startled if you have no frame of reference or context for that fee.

Unfortunately, someone who believes that he or she takes— or is capable of taking—good photographs has a difficult time accepting the fact that paying a professional photographer $1,000 or more per day is not only common but also probably a bargain. By getting cost or fee estimates from several photographers, you can get a good sense of what professional quality work can run and plan your budget accordingly.

Realistically not everyone will have a sufficient budget to afford the quality photography required to make the best impression. In such cases, attempt to persuade a competent photographer to reduce his or her fee in exchange for some publicity, such as prominent photo credits.

68. CHECK-TEST TO DETERMINE THAT THE PUBLICITY PHOTOS YOU ARE ABOUT TO TAKE ARE WHAT YOU NEED TO HELP YOU "SELL" YOUR MESSAGE.

Photographers typically take Polaroid test photos prior to taking the actual photographs you will use. To the photographer, the test photos are to make certain that light, shadows, reflections, distractions, and other variable elements are what they must be to assure a good photo.

The publicist should check these test photos to make certain that the shot is what is wanted or needed. It is common to see a picture in one's mind that doesn't materialize in the photo—in part, because the photographer can't see into the publicist's mind. The test photos afford an opportunity to alter positions, change expressions, introduce a prop, or in some way add strength, energy, or a spark to make the photographs as good as they need to be.

69. NONPROFESSIONALS CAN BENEFIT FROM PROFESSIONAL EQUIPMENT.

There will be situations, of course, where, no matter how much the publicist begs and pleads for the budget to engage a fine professional photographer, the funds just won't be available. Often the publicist will be called upon to create the publicity photos or to utilize the services of a nonprofessional photographer. In such situations the publicist should attempt to compensate for the possible lack of experience or talent by using the best equipment available. The equipment might be borrowed or rented to make the best of the situation.

70. THINK OF PUBLICITY PHOTOGRAPHS AS THEY WILL APPEAR IN PRINT.

That plant on the desk looks great, but will it look like a gray blob in the newspaper? The pattern of classic Burmese postage stamps on the CEO's necktie is a work of art, but will it appear to be a series of jagged smears in the brochure?

Real life and the camera's viewfinder can present quite a different effect from that of a newspaper photo that has been photocopied and faxed to an editor or a program chairman. As with the text message, less is more. Keep photo elements, structure, and composition simple and uncomplicated.

As the standard publicity photo is a 5" × 7" or an 8" × 10" black-and-white print, think of what this basic photo will show, and stay as close to the basics as possible. Getting fancy or flashy with photos to "dress up" the press kit is fine, as long as this is *in addition to* the basic publicity photo and not *in place of it.*

71. CHECK TO DETERMINE WHETHER YOUR MEDIA'S DEADLINE FOR PHOTOGRAPHS IS THE SAME AS OR DIFFERENT FROM THE DEADLINE FOR TEXT INFORMATION.

Typically a daily newspaper's photo deadlines are earlier than copy deadlines to allow for photo layouts and production. Obviously deadlines will vary from publication to publication and may be quite different for television. This is not a major concern in the case of radio publicity.

72. DETERMINE WHO OWNS THE RIGHTS TO PHOTOGRAPHS BEFORE THEY ARE USED FOR PUBLICITY PURPOSES.

This is not as obvious as it might seem. A company or client, having paid the photographer's fee and all processing charges and produced the prints, may assume that it owns the photographs, negatives, and empty boxes the rolls of film came in. The photographer typically believes that, as the photographs are a reflection and the result of his or her talent, they are the property of the photographer.

Forbes magazine could not grant the right to reproduce a cover of an issue of its own magazine, as it determined the cover to be largely photographic art, and that was the property of a free-lance photographer who was hired to create the cover photo.

The product "Elizabeth Taylor's White Diamonds perfume" uses an ad and promotional literature in which the contents are the copyrighted property of Parfums International, while the "image" of Elizabeth Taylor is owned by the actress, but the *photograph* that conveys the image is owned by the photographer. No information was available about who owned the punctuation marks in the material.

When employing the services of freelancers, be aware of applicable copyright laws that protect art, photography, and writing. Make certain the matter is resolved in writing prior to the publicity photos being put to use, or you may well find yourself limited in how you may use a photograph of your company, your product, or yourself.

73. Make certain that proper permits and approvals have been arranged before gathering or taking photographs of public or private property.

The expression "It's a free country" doesn't mention anything about permit fees. It is fairly common knowledge that people are often not allowed to gather on public land without first obtaining a permit. Presumably this relates to health and safety considerations. But few people are aware that permission must also be granted before one can photograph someone giving a talk in the doorway of the Library of Congress and any number of public or semipublic buildings. Gathering for virtually any purpose in Yellowstone National Park requires similar approval.

One cannot simply decide to hold a press conference in a public school, even though it is a public building, nor create a photo opportunity in the lobby of virtually any "city hall" in any city in the United States. This is not to say that such sites are unavailable, merely that permission must be sought. Assuming the location will not be used for blatantly commercial, unlawful, or obscene purposes, permission is likely to be granted. Just as a release or permission must be granted before an individual's likeness can be used in public, be aware that in many cases the rights to use "public" property or likenesses of it must similarly be secured.

74. Make certain that the media understand which, if any, interviews, placements, photographs, or other materials or data are offered on an exclusive basis and which are for general release.

Editors at more than a few publications have been angered and/or annoyed at believing that they had been given information no one else had or that they had at least been given a head start over competing publications, by the source of the information, only to see the material appear at or before the time they ran with the story. Managing the flow of information is good. Manipulating members of the media so that they will never return your phone calls again is not good. Be clear about what is an exclusive piece of information and what is not.

75. Have an objective or disinterested person review press releases, backgrounders, fact sheets, and other materials.

It is certainly in order to have an expert or authority on your subject review your material for accuracy before releasing it to the public. It is just as important to have a nonexpert review the material to ask the simple or obvious questions about it. This is a check to assure clarity and readability, as well as a discipline to avoid trade jargon and unclear or inside references that do not in any way advance your publicity objective.

76. Proofread your material *before* it goes out.

Despite the fact that so many truly great newspapers, books, and magazines have gone out to the world with misspellings, typos, and grammatical mistakes, there is no reason for treating your own material with an indifferent or cavalier attitude. You are trying to win support for your subject from the media and the public. Be concise and to the point, and make certain, to the degree that it is possible, to check for errors that might distract from the subject or otherwise leave a less-than-favorable impression. Remember that the last person who shrugged and said, "Yeah, we always check that stuff" probably is with the paper in which you found the typo this morning.

77. PREPARE FOR INTERVIEWS, LOOK READY, *BE* READY.

It is said that in 1960, Vice President Richard Nixon arrived at the television studio where he was to debate Senator John F. Kennedy and, while looking tired and pale, felt confident of his knowledge of the subject of the debate and of his ability to get the better of his opponent. Senator Kennedy, on the other hand, was said to have prepared for the debate as a student might study for a final exam. He also chose a dark suit that would help him to stand out and look better against a gray backdrop and on black-and-white television. History says most people believe John Kennedy won that debate. He *looked* better and clearly had a keen grasp of the issues.

Though your subject is likely not preparing for a presidential debate, a lot can still be learned from the Nixon-Kennedy experience: Be prepared.

In terms of wardrobe, consider what your interviewer might be wearing. The reason for this is that, as the subject of an interview, you want to neither underdress nor overdress relative to your questioner.

Sound stupid? Consider this: as a senior executive or spokesperson for your subject, you (or your boss, your client, or your designated spokesperson) should present a look and an image of success. Such an image does not come from looking as if you slept in your car the night before. Look sharp. However, it is not necessary to look so sharp that the interviewer feels uncomfortable because you are wearing a suit that cost more than he or she earns in a month. This does happen. Dress sharp, but tastefully, and remember that a touch of understatement tends to play better than overstatement.

On the seemingly more substantive side, prepare for the interview by reviewing the subjects about which the reporter is likely to ask, as well as any controversial or "hot" questions that may come up, and prepare a list of "talking points": those you want to be sure to cover, or at least reference, in the interview. Keep the list close at hand, and do not be self-conscious about referring to it if you must.

Keep your comments and responses to questions fairly brief. The shorter and more concise the comments, the more likely they are to be both quoted and quoted accurately.

Rehearsal is a form of preparation. Some people "role-play" the interviewer beforehand as a form of rehearsal. Some audiotape the rehearsal and listen to the tapes to determine whether or not they are comfortable with their responses.

Some people videotape these rehearsals and check for eye contact, hand gestures, body language, overall presentation, neatness, and aptness of thought (the last two points being among the criteria from the Miss America pageant). Seeing oneself on tape for the first time in such a situation can be a revealing or an unsettling experience, but helpful.

There is a reason why certain people look so well groomed and well prepared during interviews; they are.

78. USE "SOUND BITES."

Sound bites are brief comments—sometimes colorful, poetic, or outrageous—specifically constructed to be quoted, represented as well-chosen points or sentiments. Inspiring, irreverent, ironic, insightful, smart, or stinging, these are comments that qualify as irresistible and too good for the media not to report.

79. BE CAREFUL IN THE CHOICE OF A DESIGNATED SPOKESPERSON.

Your spokesperson must be well informed as to the facts of the
subject but must also appear sincere, easily understood, and capable of bringing the subject sharply into focus. Spokespersons who
are too "slick" invite suspicion, as well as distract from the essence
of the subject. Be careful if your spokesperson is a celebrity or
otherwise well-known individual whose presence may overshadow
the subject.

80. REVIEW YOUR PRESENTATION ON TAPE.

Whether your priority is delivering a speech, giving an interview,
appearing on a talk show, or just becoming more comfortable with
the subject and your ability to explain it, audiotape and, if possible, videotape your remarks. Review the tape carefully with someone unfamiliar with the subject, to determine both *what* is being
said and *how* it is being said.

   Check if there are any "holes" in your presentation—any
obvious omissions. Get a sense of how your message plays. Check
your body language. These are the things your audience—whether
a single interviewer, a roomful of executives, or a television camera—will be taking note of, often as much as the content of what
you have to say.

   It is increasingly common for a writer to report, following a
press conference, a speech, or an interview, that the speaker looked
tired or distracted or annoyed and failed to make note of . . . whatever. Being well prepared is important, but being comfortable with
the material being presented and *how* it is being presented is equally
important in that your publicity, in the form of media coverage, will
reflect this.

81. DO NOT READ A SPEECH OR A PREPARED STATEMENT—UNLESS YOU
HAVE TO.

Delivering a speech, publicizing it before and after it is delivered,
and including highlights of its best passages are excellent and

highly effective publicity devices. The advice to speakers for almost as long as there have been podiums is that speeches should not be read. The theory behind this advice is that:

1. A speaker who reads the speech must not be very familiar with its contents and, therefore, is not very knowledgeable on the subject.
2. Reading a speech is discourteous to the audience and conveys a lack of honesty if the speaker can't make eye contact with the people being addressed.
3. In terms of overall presentation, reading a speech simply *looks bad.*

Maybe. There is little question that a person who can deliver a well-organized speech of considerable substance, without benefit of notes, is regarded as impressive and conveys a sense of competence. These are rather important things to convey when the objective is to generate good publicity.

But some people can no more deliver a speech without notes —either "off-the-cuff" or from memory—than they can sing or take the lead in *Hamlet.* Delivering a good speech without reading it is a talent, even if it is a learned talent. Not everyone can do it, nor should someone be taken to task for lacking that particular skill if knowledge and competence are present.

Recognizing that an audience does in fact respond better to a speech that is delivered as if it were a great performance (though, of course it cannot *appear* to be a performance), a speaker should try to deliver his or her piece without reading it. If, however, that's not going to work—perhaps for no reason other than the speaker is uncomfortable being put in that situation—the best advice is to go ahead and read it. Presenting its substance is more important than demonstrating the speaker's acting skill.

Further, the speaker can confront the subject head-on by simply prefacing his or her remarks with, "I apologize for having to read this speech, but I want to be sure that I don't leave out something important." Given that publicity is the goal, ultimately it is better to be regarded as a good source of information than as a good performer.

Regarding a prepared statement, to read it may seem more "official" whereas to not read it may cause it to appear informal or "off-the-cuff." Decide which impression you want to convey.

82. Visualize how the media will treat your presentation.

This is not an exercise in New Age thinking; it is another step in presenting your information—whether it is a speech, press release, video, or report—in a form that has both style and substance.

Put yourself in the place of the media to which you are directing your material, and act as the "reviewer." If your review includes statements such as "It ran a little long," then cut some of it. The additional information can always be presented in supporting documents, handouts, or accompanying fact sheets or other documents or tapes.

If a reviewer might describe your material as "light on specifics," add some specifics. The media respond very positively to numbers: costs, dates, budgets, savings, or overruns. If the material might be termed "dry," lighten it up with a historic reference or two, or insert a relevant quote to break up the "heaviness" of the piece. There are volumes of quotes from Woody Allen to Voltaire that are designed for just such entertaining and educational purposes. The media may not compare your remarks to those of Shakespeare or Churchill, but it probably won't hurt to drop a hint.

83. Research the media in which you want to appear before contacting them.

It is fairly common for a client or employer to say, "I'd like to see this story make the trades" and then go on to frame the story in a way that the trade press would never do it. Preparing a story for presentation to the media and wishful thinking are not the same

thing. Before contacting those on your list of targeted media, read
the newspapers, magazines, newsletters, and journals, watch and
listen to the programs you are contacting, and become familiar
with styles and formats—not only *what* they do but also *how* they
do it. Present your story to them in ways that will make them
most receptive to using it.

While a general press release or a fairly general, all-inclusive
media kit is fine, one size does not fit all in media circles. Experienced publicists understand that the approach used to interest
the *New York Times Sunday Magazine* will not be the same as the
approach to "Securities Week," even if the two have a significant
overlap in readership. The worst words for a publicist to hear
from a reporter, a columnist, an editor, or a producer are "Do
you have any idea what it is we do here?" Look first and have
an idea.

84. KEEP THE FOCUS ON YOUR SUBJECT.

Instant global communication has made many company chiefs
and their publicists believe that every subject must be broad, all-
encompassing, and global in scope. A concert on the mall is still
a concert on the mall, and the opening of the new women's health
center is just exactly that, regardless of what implications others
may attach to it. Consider such implications in preparing your
message, but to try to anticipate and address too much dilutes the
basic message and distracts from the focus of the message.

Anticipate what, if any, criticism or negative response your
message might invite, and address such concerns to the degree it
is necessary. But avoid the tendency to react to criticism in ways
that focus more attention on the criticism than on your subject.

85. USE "FORMULA" FORMATS TO ACHIEVE PUBLICITY.

Both the media and the public respond to what can be termed
"formula" formats: problem/solution; need/fulfillment; action/
reaction. Experiment with ways to present your message within

such formats that may create interest on the part of otherwise disinterested media.

86. EMPHASIZE THE BENEFITS TO BOTH GENERAL AND SPECIFIC
AUDIENCES IN WHAT YOUR MESSAGE CONVEYS.

The fact that you have a message that you want to publicize is not newsworthy, but what benefits and advantages your message may present to the audience does have interest and value. While staying focused on—and emphasizing—*your* subject message, opportunities for publicity are increased by the number of ways your subject can be shown to have value to others.

For example, announcing that your company has created a new product that can heal rough, damaged, infected hands can be a strong general-interest story, but it can also be an important trade story to *many different trades* in how it has particular value to auto mechanics, factory workers, construction workers, hospital staff, and food-service personnel, to name a few. The more fine-tuning of your story that can reveal more groups that will benefit, the more opportunities for publicity can be identified.

87. VIDEO NEWS RELEASES SHOULD LOOK LIKE NEWS.

Just as a press release should be written enough like a news story (who, what, when, where, why, and how) to fit into a newspaper, a video news release should look as if it is comparable to any other news or feature story using videotape on a television newscast.

VNRs are typically produced to, of course, show the subject at its best visually, but also to show product demonstrations, highlights of an event, or a display that a television station would not likely go out to cover but might feature if a tape were somehow provided.

VNRs have gained popularity in secondary markets and on second-tier TV stations in major markets, where budgets routinely are tight. Good-quality VNRs are not inexpensive to produce and, as such, are not widely produced or distributed by publicists operating on modest budgets.

In terms of content, again, news department standards apply. VNRs are not television commercials, and many television stations screen these tapes extra carefully to make certain that TV commercial material is not being recycled or incorporated into them, disguised as visuals in a news story.

88. CHOOSE A GOOD LOCATION OR BACKDROP FOR YOUR PUBLICITY EFFORT.

The Rose Garden of the White House is a great place to make an announcement. For that matter, virtually any rose garden is a lovely setting for an announcement. There is a good reason why candidates do not announce their candidacy from the living rooms of their homes and why politicians choose to meet the press from the steps of the Lincoln Memorial, their local statehouses, or the site of something great and historical. For television cameras and still photographers, a visually stunning or powerful location or backdrop frames a subject much more interestingly than a blank wall. For print journalists—or even for the press release itself—to report that the subject was presented at the site of a new office tower, on the banks of a local river, on the steps of a local high school, at a center for senior citizens, in an ice-cream parlor, at a factory gate, and so forth, conveys a sense of imagery that gives focus and energy to the presentation of a message.

The nature of your subject and the objective of your publicity effort will dictate which are the logical available choices. As your campaign or program progresses, alternate between highly visible and familiar sites for announcements, activities, and photo opportunities, and more mainstream sites such as hotel conference settings.

For the initial announcement or launch of your publicity effort, if at all possible, choose a popular, prominent, landmark, historic, or otherwise familiar setting that maximizes the opportunity for your message to receive publicity, as opposed to a more neutral setting.

89. BLOCK, PACE, AND TIME PRESENTATIONS AND SPEECHES.

Speeches and presentations are best structured into "units" of 10 to 20 seconds if you are hoping to receive media attention. As many as possible of these units should contain a quotable reference or sound bite that can be used in a radio or television piece or easily be quoted in its self-contained entirety by print reporters.

While dropping as many such units as possible into interviews or conversations with reporters is fine (until it looks so obvious and appears that the speaker is too well rehearsed and incapable of a spontaneous thought), the real best place for them is in a television or radio interview, or in a speech of which copies will be distributed for media use.

Editors appreciate not having to burrow through tapes of entire speeches looking for an excerpt to quote and laboring to edit it down to manageable length.

90. DO NOT ALLOW THE PRESENTER OF YOUR SUBJECT TO OVERSHADOW YOUR SUBJECT OR MESSAGE.

Nuances that define the culture have changed. Andy Warhol's amusing reference to everybody's 15 minutes of fame has become somewhat dated. Since the advent of cable television, nearly everyone fully expects that the 15 minutes will soon turn into his or her own cable television show.

CEOs don't just tell what's ahead for the corporations they lead, but discuss their families, their hobbies, and their personal ambitions. Dr. Freud would have been fascinated. Film producers who used to give newspaper, magazine, and TV interviews, talking about their films, now talk about themselves. A reporter writing a book about a famous murder trial made the book as much about himself as it was about the trial. The public seems as comfortable hearing a TV chef tell about getting a speeding ticket as about getting the recipe.

All this might be fine down the road, but to generate good publicity for a subject, attention must remain on the subject.

Having a celebrity spokesperson has its advantages certainly, but one can note disadvantages as well. Surveys indicate that much of the public think Dick Clark and Ed McMahon were spokesmen for the Publishers' Clearing House sweepstakes, when actually it was that of a rival magazine publishers' enterprise, the American Family sweepstakes. Speaking of Ed McMahon, with all due respect, he is also known as a spokesman for a mail-order insurance company; no one can remember the name of that one either. To get publicity for the subject, let the subject, its benefits, and its unique selling points be the star of the story.

91. Know *whom* to approach in the media.

Just as it is important to keep very up-to-date media lists, knowing whom to approach is important. Unless you have just received a Pulitzer Prize and an Oscar, don't bother calling Larry King to get a spot on the *Larry King Show* on CNN. That goes double for Oprah Winfrey, Tom Snyder, Charlie Rose, Regis Philbin, or any other host.

Television and radio programs have producers, associate producers, assistant producers, and bookers who consider, pre-interview, and confirm guests and subjects. Despite this fact's being fairly widely known for years, hosts of television and radio programs continue to receive calls and letters from publicists and nonpublicists, announcing they've ". . . got the perfect guest for your show."

Suffice to say, depending on their prominence, some callers are treated more courteously than others. Calling a host is not a way to book guests. Check appropriate media directories, or call the show's production office and ask for the name of the producer, to whom letters, releases, and tapes should be messengered.

92. Know *how* to approach . . .

Even though publicists are salespeople, when it comes to contacting the media to generate publicity by pitching a story and/or guest or spokesperson to present its message, publicists are not telemarketers.

Review the list of targeted media; know whom to contact; know about the publication or program, its format and criteria, its closing dates, deadlines, lead time, and material production requirements; know what each of them is currently looking for, and tailor your presentation as close to that as possible without in any way compromising your subject.

93. CLEARLY IDENTIFY YOUR *HOOKS*.

Editors and producers look for timeliness, uniqueness, value, and human interest in subjects they choose to cover. That yours is a profitable manufacturing company in Georgia is not a news hook that merits publicity. The fact that 70 percent of your employees are second-generation employees might be. That more than half of your employees are on a flextime program to help them fit their jobs in around their families is good too. Don't make the media have to look hard and deep to find your subject message; define it clearly and quickly, emphasizing the advantages to the audience.

94. PUT ENERGY INTO YOUR MESSAGE.

The local newspaper received a notice that the guest speaker at the next luncheon program of the Civic Club would be speaking on *replacement cost accounting.*

The publicist needn't wait to hear someone yell, "Stop the presses—hold the back page!" While the topic may be useful, important, and even stimulating (especially with lunch) to any number of audience members, it is not a subject likely to entice a reporter to cover the luncheon, much less to bring along a photographer. The same program with a title such as "Yesterday's Managers with Today's Money Look at Tomorrow's Business" might have attracted a bit more interest.

It is never a good idea to attract the media's attention with smoke and mirrors, but if a subject is going to attract interest, it must at least *sound* interesting.

95. MAKE YOUR SUBJECT APPEAL TO AS MANY OF THE SENSES AS POSSIBLE.

To generate publicity, the key elements are focusing on the unique selling points (USPs), emphasizing benefits to the public, and working a finely tuned media list aggressively—sending material and following up. Certainly beyond that, various approaches that make the subject seem more interesting and worthy of attention are those that appeal to the senses: strong visuals, accompanying music or a strong audio message, a brochure, or premiums to take away as a desktop or wall-mounted reminder of the subject.

96. TEST PRESENTATION EQUIPMENT IN ADVANCE.

After much consideration, the press conference was called and the best media were on hand to cover it. The speaker straightened up and announced into the microphone, "If I may direct your attention to the screen on my left . . ." as all eyes turned and waited patiently for . . . nothing. The machine didn't work, or the tape wasn't properly positioned—or wasn't there at all. There was awkward scrambling as everyone waited for the speaker to try to figure out what went wrong; he finally gave up and began to explain to the assembled group how the subject was worthy of their attention.

In another presentation, the same speaker revealed to a different group that he had indeed brought the wrong tape, but if he'd had the right tape, here's what it would have told them . . .

A blown projector bulb, microphones that don't work, or a VCR with a temperamental speaker wire may all be par for the course, but in a public meeting, with representatives of the press in attendance, these are costly mistakes that end up in the newspaper ("The speaker, who said all the information he wanted to present was on a videotape that, unfortunately, he couldn't seem to access . . .").

Whether you provide your own equipment or use that provided by meeting facilities, check it out before you need to use it. Don't let faulty equipment lose you an opportunity to publicize your message.

97. ANTICIPATE QUESTIONS, COMMENTS, AND CHALLENGES.

Your publicity effort is not a one-way flow of communication. Interviews are questions. Press conferences, as well as the 15 minutes after a speech, are times when people will often feel compelled to challenge your premise, or ask you to support your conclusions or prove statistics you've quoted by citing research that can be reviewed. Be prepared.

98. CALL PEOPLE BY NAME, AND PUT NAMES OF PEOPLE AND PLACES INTO YOUR PRESENTATION; LOCALIZE AND PERSONALIZE YOUR MESSAGE TO THE EXTENT YOU CAN.

As members of the audience want to feel that they're not hearing a "canned" or "generic" speech, attempt to work the names of familiar people and places into your interviews, press conferences, and speeches. It helps to promote a more personal connection between the audience and the speaker.

President Bill Clinton has been shown at his best in "town hall" meetings, speaking directly to individuals, reaching out and touching a shoulder or an arm and making eye contact. Although his words were for the larger audience, individuals felt he was speaking personally to them. His critics have labeled it phony and theatrical, but the audience loved it—and left the building loving him. Getting publicity is spreading your message. The people in your audience prefer not to be thought of as an audience. They are individuals, and to the extent you can make your message "connect" with each one, you will have a partner who will help to spread your message.

99. PROMOTE YOUR PUBLICITY.

Develop a database. Send copies of your best press clippings to names on your list. Include the best of your publicity clips in your media kit. Don't assume that the entire target audience you are trying to reach saw that great story about you in the *Times*. Bring it to their attention in any way you can.

100. Do the unexpected.

There may not be a company or a business around that doesn't like to think that it does something "a little differently." Most of them don't. Most business enterprises pretty much follow standard rules. It is for this reason that the company that creates on-site day care for its employees, or keeps people on well after what competitors consider the mandatory retirement age, or has a gourmet chef in the company cafeteria, or provides free shuttle transportation for customers and employees, or offers lunchtime classes for employees in foreign languages, musical artistry, or band, or for-credit courses toward an uncompleted degree . . . makes news.

A free buffet table for clients of your stereo store or auto repair business or clinic, valet parking or child care . . . Doing things a little differently gets noticed.

101. Do the expected.

While others are scrambling to be different, embrace stability and consistency. Reward employees for long service. Create incentives to keep people happy. Have a "bounce-back" card with a prize catalog that rewards customers for coming back year after year.

And tell all about it. The people who get quoted in newspapers and magazines, invited to talk shows, and are always introduced as "the experts" are those who *offered* their opinions, often unsolicited. Check the daily papers, the newswires, and the Internet, and as often as possible, offer a comment on the wires or in the form of a Monday-morning ("what's ahead") or Friday-morning ("week in review") press release.

Some will call you an opportunist. Others will say *shameless* opportunist.

Many will wonder why *you* are always the one being quoted on behalf of your product, subject, or company and why you are getting so much publicity.

The answer may be as simple as *they had to notice you because you were blocking their view.*

Bibliography

Advertising Age: "For Ford and GM, loyalty in the cards," by Gary Levin, March 28, 1994.

Chicago Tribune: "Field Days," November 16, 1997; November 30, 1997.

Madison Avenue U.S.A., by Martin Mayer, NTC Business Books, 1992.

Media Guide: A Critical Review of the Media, edited by Jude Wanniski, Polyconomics, 1990.

New Publicity Kit, by Jeanette Smith, John Wiley & Sons, 1995.

New York Times: "Success in Failures," by Martin Stolz, January 19, 1998; "Ad Bowl Serves Up Chips, Both Snack and Computer," by Stuart Elliott, January 23, 1998; Lord & Taylor Christmas Carol, November 16, 1997; "Peace Is an Art," November 16, 1997.

New York Times Magazine: "Looking for an 11 o'clock Fix," by Michael Winerip, January 11, 1998.

Publicity and Public Relations, by Dorothy I. Doty, Barron's Educational Services, 1990.

Shock Marketing, by Joe Marconi, Bonus Books, 1997.

Spin Control, by John Anthony Maltese, University of North Carolina Press, 1992.

Index

About the Author

Joe Marconi is a marketing communications consultant and writer with more than two decades of award-winning advertising, public relations, and marketing programs to his credit. He has been both a corporate communications executive and principal of a major national agency.

A frequent lecturer and marketing communications seminar leader throughout the United States and Canada, his writing has appeared in numerous publications, including the *International Herald Tribune,* the *Chicago Tribune, Marketing News,* and *American Demographics* magazine. He is the author of five previous books: *Getting the Best from Your Ad Agency; Beyond Branding; Shock Marketing; Advertising, Influence, and Family Values; Image Marketing;* and *Crisis Marketing: When Bad Things Happen to Good Companies.* He is also the editor of *The Marketing Communications Executive Summary,* a twice-monthly newsletter.

Joe lives in Western Springs, Illinois, near Chicago.